This journal
has been kept by:

....

from: ....

to: ....

If found please contact:

....

THRIVE
WHERE
YOU'RE
PLANTED

A GUIDED JOURNAL

to Help You Connect with the

Natural Wonders in Your Neighborhood

Written by Andrea Debbink

QUIRK BOOKS
PHILADELPHIA

CONTENTS

INTRODUCTION

Nature can seem far away—especially in the city. I grew up in the suburbs and have lived in apartments my whole adult life, so I understand the temptation to think that a wilder world lies beyond the city limits. The natural and the human-made can be at odds here in our urban and suburban spaces: trees are cleared for new construction, traffic noise drowns out birdsong, and streetlights blot out all but the brightest stars.

But nature can also seem far away because of the limited way we define it. In the collective imagination, nature is a vacation destination, not the fluttering, blooming, unkempt reality that sprouts through pavement and wings its way through superstore parking lots. We revere national parks while overlooking and undervaluing everyday nature—the wild plants, creatures, and worlds thriving in the urban and suburban places where so many of us live.

Yet it's here. Nature's wonders are nearer than most city dwellers realize. A vacant lot can have as much biodiversity as a patch of forest. Some animal species—such as coyotes and gray squirrels—thrive in urban environments. Every backyard garden, street tree, and wildflower-sprouting median counts as nature, and each is one more way we can experience the natural world if we're willing.

This is a guided journal for people who want to find peace and joy in the natural wonders that await in ordinary places. The process is simple and moves at the pace of the seasons: the journal is divided into spring, summer, autumn, and winter, with a chapter for each month. It's best to start the journal at the beginning of a season, but you can also start with the current month. Don't forget to refer to the Resources section on page 207 for books and apps that will help you identify plants, animals, and celestial phenomena.

No matter when you begin using it, I hope that as you explore nature in the year ahead, this guided journal will sharpen your senses so that you can find nature right where you are and see the magic in the ordinary.

EACH SEASON INCLUDES THREE MONTH-LONG CHAPTERS THAT CONTAIN THE FOLLOWING SECTIONS

Field Notes: Read an essay on a seasonal nature topic to help ground you in each month.

Discover: This section provides ways to engage more deeply in the season or the natural features of your neighborhood.

Read the Sky: This section includes a weather tracker chart and describes what you can see in the sky each month, including cloud types, constellations, and planets.

Flora and Fauna: This section describes seasonal changes in the plant and animal worlds and provides space for you to record your own observations.

Taste the Wild: This section describes wild edibles that can be foraged throughout North America and includes a table where you can track your discoveries. Although foragers need to take extra precautions in cities, urban foraging is growing in popularity and there are many great resources that can help you in your search (see page 207).

Bring Nature Near: This section provides practical ideas on how to bring the wild into your everyday life if nature is hard to find where you live.

Notes from My Natural Habitat: Visit the same place in nature each month and record your observations and thoughts in this section. Before getting started, see "Find Your Place in Nature" on page 6.

Be Rooted: Mindfulness involves paying attention to the present moment. Each month, this is where you'll find a brief nature-based mindfulness practice to try.

Poem: Nature has long been the muse of poets, and poetry communicates things about nature that prose can't. Each month ends with a seasonal poem to inspire you, followed by space to write your own.

A FEW NOTES BEFORE YOU BEGIN

FIND YOUR PLACE IN NATURE

Exploring new locations in the outdoors has its merits, but there's something special about having a home base, a place in nature that you can return to again and again. Most naturalists have had their favorite haunts (think of Henry David Thoreau and Walden Pond); there's no reason you shouldn't have one too. The most important consideration is proximity. It'll be easiest if you choose a place that's near your home or relatively easy for you to reach: a local park or churchyard, your own yard or porch, or even the view of the street from your bedroom window. The idea is to select a spot you can visit at least once a month and observe nature. You can record your observations in the "Notes from My Natural Habitat" sections in this journal each month. Jot down some information about the place you've chosen below.

MY PLACE IN NATURE

Where it is:

....

....

Why I chose it:

....

....

My favorite time to visit this place *(circle one)*:

MORNING   AFTERNOON   EVENING   NIGHT

FORAGE WISELY AND TREAD LIGHTLY

Foraging is becoming a popular activity in suburbs and cities and can be a hands-on way to learn about local plant life. That said, foraging can also harm the environment—and the person who's foraging—when it's not done responsibly. If you choose to forage wild edibles, here are some important guidelines.

- Only forage for plants in areas where it's legal to do so. It's important to know a property's rules about foraging before picking plants or collecting wild edibles.

- Never pick a plant unless you're certain of its identity. Many plant species are legally protected. There are also many plants that are toxic to humans, even fatally so, and the plant world is full of lookalikes.

- Never eat a plant unless you're certain of its identity—*and* know the correct way to prepare it. There are plants that shouldn't be eaten raw but become digestible once they're cooked.

- Avoid foraging in areas that have been sprayed with chemicals like fertilizers and pesticides.

- Take only a small amount of any wild edible you find. Every plant is a part of the ecosystem, and there are creatures and other organisms that need the plant in order to survive and thrive.

For more information, check out the foraging resources listed on page 207.

March

"A birdsong can even, for a moment, make the whole world into a sky within us, because we feel that the bird does not distinguish between its heart and the world's."

—Rainer Maria Rilke

THE DAWN CHORUS

On spring mornings, I feel like a botanist seeking a rare plant hidden in the green folds of the day. I wake early, searching for quiet, a clearing in the thorny underbrush of suburban sound where something more delicate can take root. The finch practicing his solo. The invisible insects tuning their strings like a tiny orchestra. The mourning dove's haunting call. I often miss it. Too soon, the quiet is crowded out. If the clearing is there at all, by seven a.m. I can no longer find it, and nature's music is tangled up in the world's noise.

Noisemakers are early risers too. The lawn around our apartment building must be cut, and the mowers shred the morning silence along with the grass. The garbage truck lurches into the parking lot. Restless dogs bark on balconies. At the edge of a growing city, there's always a construction site within earshot; another apartment complex that can't be built without bulldozers, excavators, and, apparently, a lone truck forever beeping in reverse.

The rarity of natural quiet in my city-dwelling life has taught me its value. And in my years of seeking it, I've learned where it hides: at the beginning of each day. So I wake early when I can, to experience the world that belongs to the birds. The Swedes have a word for this: *gökotta*. Roughly translated, it means "the act of waking early to listen to birdsong." As far as I know, English doesn't have a word for this activity. In American culture, we wake early to squeeze in extra work or go to the gym—not listen to robins. But maybe we'd all be better off if we did.

Birdsong isn't only pretty background noise; it's also good for us. Poets have long understood that nature is a tonic for the human soul. Science, at long last, is catching up to poetry. Scientists can now measure nature's effects on our brains and bodies, unraveling some of the reasons *why* nature is a tonic. For instance, now we know the sounds of water and wind are soothing because they increase alpha waves in our brains–similar to meditation's effects–leading to a more relaxed mental state. And there is a third natural sound that has this restorative and calming effect: birdsong.

Scientists at the University of Surrey in England have studied the benefits of birdsong for years. Their research has revealed that birdsong, more than other natural sounds, improves a person's sense of well-being and their ability to focus. Similar findings have come from researchers at California Polytechnic State University, who sought to understand why time spent in nature seemed to lower people's stress and improve their moods. They zeroed in on birdsong and found that people who listened to seven to ten minutes of it each day reported a greater sense of well-being than those who didn't.

If you live in an area where birds are scarce, you can still experience this avian nature therapy. First, you can try bringing the birds to you by hanging a birdfeeder where you can see it. If that doesn't work, listening to recorded bird calls produces the same positive effects. So close your eyes, cue the morning robins on your smartphone, and pretend you're in a forest. Spring migration is an ideal time to practice gökotta. As millions of birds cross continents and claim territories, they raise their voices. In my neighborhood, the mourning doves are the first to sing. The first one appears on a gray morning in March, its lonely call breaking the winter silence at last.

It's a toss-up as to who joins the avian chorus next. The sociable chickadees find their spring voices again. Then come the determined red-winged blackbirds, who don't mind that their pond nurseries still shine with ice. Rosy-faced house finches are next, followed by one of spring's most familiar sights, the robin. By late spring, the chorus is complete.

For me, gökotta has another benefit besides brain waves. When I listen to birds, their voices become familiar. They are no longer strangers, but my wildlife neighbors. Some people will follow the poet's call into nature, others will follow the scientist. I suppose that, in the end, it doesn't matter what compels you to listen to the chickadee on a spring morning, only that you do.

Spring is an ideal time to meet (or rediscover) the birds that live in your neighborhood. No matter where you live, most places have birds that are year-round residents, birds that are seasonal residents as they breed and raise young, and birds that are brief visitors as they migrate. The abundance of food sources in cities and suburbs has changed the migration behavior of some birds; despite changing seasons, some species may stay in these areas if there's food.

On pages 13–15, describe any birds you see in your yard, from your window, in your neighborhood, or in a park. It's OK if you don't know what species they are yet. Bird identification can be tricky, even for experienced birders.

Once you've gathered clues about some local birds, use a field guide, app, or website to identify them and learn their songs and calls. (See the Resources section on page 207 for recommendations.)

Bird name or description:

....

Where did you see the bird?

....

What was the bird doing?

....

How did its size compare to an American robin? *(circle one)*

LARGER   SMALLER   SAME

Color(s): ....

Sketch the bird:

Write down any other observations or thoughts about the bird:

....

....

....

....

Bird name or description:

....

Where did you see the bird?

....

What was the bird doing?

....

How did its size compare to an American robin? *(circle one)*

LARGER   SMALLER   SAME

Color(s): ....

Sketch the bird:

Write down any other observations or thoughts about the bird:

....

....

....

....

Bird name or description:

....

Where did you see the bird?

....

What was the bird doing?

....

How did its size compare to an American robin? *(circle one)*

LARGER   SMALLER   SAME

Color(s): ....

Sketch the bird:

Write down any other observations or thoughts about the bird:

....

....

....

....

WEATHER TRACKER

Use the following chart to keep track of weather phenomena this month. First, create a key by coloring in the dots at the bottom of the page, using a different color for each circle. Then use this color-coded system to record each day's weather. Many days will have more than one type of weather.

SUNNY   CLOUDY   PARTLY CLOUDY   WINDY
◯   ◯   ◯   ◯

RAINY   STORMY   SNOWY   FOGGY
◯   ◯   ◯   ◯

SPRING EQUINOX

The spring equinox, or the first day of spring, can occur on March 19, 20, or 21 in the northern hemisphere. On that date, day and night are of nearly equal length after months of longer nights than days. This month, celebrate the spring equinox by watching the sunrise or sunset. Record the date of this year's spring equinox and the date's sunrise and sunset times below.

Date: _____ Sunrise time: _____ Sunset time: _____

Full Moon

A moonrise can be an inspiring sight and is most brilliant when it occurs shortly after sunset. Write down the date of this month's full moon and the time when it will rise.

Date: _____ Time: _____

New Moon

The new moon phase is the point in the moon's monthly orbit when the moon is in shadow because it's between the Earth and the sun. This moon phase is an ideal time for stargazing because there isn't any moonlight to brighten the sky and dim the stars. Write down when the new moon occurs this month so you'll know the best time for stargazing.

Date: _____

It's human instinct to look for signs of a new season, and in spring, the plant world is full of them. What local plants do you see sprouting or blooming this month? If you don't know their names, describe them below, then use a field guide or app to identify them.

Plant name or description	Date spotted	Place spotted

QUIRK ✻ BOOKS

Hi Tsh,

I'm happy to enclose a copy of *Thrive Where You're Planted* (Quirk Books;
February 6, 2024). Author and naturalist Andrea Debbink will help you realize that
the natural world can be found even closer than you think through seasonal essays,
nature poetry, foraging tips, and journaling pages.

Feel free to email me at any time with your thoughts. I hope this mindful guided
journal brings you peace, simplicity, and allows you to slow down and connect
with the natural beauty all around you!

Happy journaling,

CLT.

Gaby Iori
Publicist and Marketing Coordinator
giori@quirkbooks.com

Record any wildlife or animal signs you see this month. Watch for events like the appearance of butterflies or the return of whales and other ocean creatures. And keep a lookout for baby animals emerging from their dens, burrows, or nests.

Creature	Date spotted	Place spotted	Activity (if applicable)

For notes on how to find your place in nature, see page 6.

Location: ....

Date & Time: ....

Weather & Temperature:..

5 Things I See:

....

....

....

....

....

3 Things I Hear:

....

....

....

1 Thing I Smell:

....

1 Thing I Feel:

....

WAKE UP WITH THE BIRDS

Choose one day this month to practice gökotta. As close to sunrise as possible, sit outside and listen to birdsong for at least five minutes. You don't have to go far: a front step, backyard, or apartment balcony will do. If you can't hear birds where you live, find a birdsong recording online to listen to. Your brain won't know the difference. Close your eyes or keep them open, but put aside distractions if you can, including your phone. Simply be present and still while you listen.

This month, sunrise is around _____ a.m.

To the Thawing Wind

by Robert Frost

Come with rain, O loud Southwester!
Bring the singer, bring the nester;
Give the buried flower a dream;
Make the settled snowbank steam;
Find the brown beneath the white;
But whate'er you do tonight,
Bathe my window, make it flow,
Melt it as the ice will go;
Melt the glass and leave the sticks
Like a hermit's crucifix;
Burst into my narrow stall;
Swing the picture on the wall;
Run the rattling pages o'er;
Scatter poems on the floor;
Turn the poet out of door.

Think about the ways you've experienced nature this month.
Pick an experience or something you observed and use it to
inspire your own poem below.

....

....

....

....

....

....

....

....

....

....

....

....

....

....

....

....

....

....

....

April

"There is something infinitely healing
in the repeated refrains of nature—
the assurance that dawn comes after
night, and spring after winter."

–Rachel Carson

CALL OF THE WILD

Not long after sunset, the howling begins. A haunting solo answered by a chorus of yips. The sounds seem out of place here among dense blocks of houses. I lean out the balcony door. Squinting into the streetlights' glare, I can't see anything, but I hear them: coyotes, howling in the deep-blue darkness. Coyotes are common in cities like mine. And like many city-dwelling animals, these canines are misunderstood, dismissed as pests or worse. But my neighborhood coyote family and their incongruous howls comfort me. They're a reminder of the wilder world that weaves together with my own.

More than a century ago, American urbanites shared my longing for nature. In mid-nineteenth-century New York City, one sighting of a lone gray squirrel drew hundreds of curious onlookers. At the time, urban wildlife was rare, after animals such as squirrels had been driven out of cities as their habitats were destroyed. By the late nineteenth century, however, East Coast cities were stocking their parks with squirrels in a bid to make urban spaces feel more like the countryside, even encouraging residents to feed these animals as though they were public pets.

But not all urban wildlife can be traced to human experiments. Some animals have simply moved back, adapting to the new environments we've created. Known as habitat generalists, these animals aren't picky about what they eat or where they live—including familiar creatures like raccoons, coyotes, opossums, and foxes. In a changing world where extinction is a serious concern for many other species, these animals are thriving. Yet not everyone admires their adaptability.

Wildlife-and-human coexistence is a notoriously thorny issue. People often react to wildlife with fear or annoyance. City animals are typically seen as creatures to trap, repel, relocate, or kill. But as biologists are learning, eradicating urban wildlife is a mistake. Wild animals are not always harmless, but we tend to exaggerate their potential danger while ignoring their benefits. We fail to see that our own human habitats wouldn't be the same without the contributions of these misunderstood creatures.

The field of urban ecology is still new. People don't always see urban-dwelling species as *real* nature. Even scientists once assumed that cities were "biological deserts." But now we know that the relationship between cities and nature is complex. City environments can be a threat to habitat and biodiversity, and yet they can also create habitat and encourage biodiversity.

Biodiversity naturally creates checks and balances. No one wants to live in a city overrun with rats. That's why animals who depend on them for food—like coyotes, hawks, and owls—should be made welcome. Likewise, mammals such as opossums and bats help control tick and mosquito populations, reducing the spread of Lyme disease and other illnesses. And many other animals—including raccoons, seagulls, and ants—clean up cities by feasting on roadkill, rotting vegetation, and food waste.

It's been two years since I heard coyotes in my neighborhood, and I wonder what's become of them. Each year in the US, more than half a million coyotes are killed by government agencies and individual citizens. Unlike other wildlife such as deer, which have specific hunting seasons and regulations, coyotes aren't protected in any way. In some states, like mine, there are even legal coyote hunts in which participants compete to hunt and kill as many coyotes as possible. The coyote's reputation as "vermin" has been hard to shake. I'm sure raccoons and opossums can empathize. But I hope that as the field of urban ecology expands, our perspective on these animals will expand too; that we will come to see them as our neighbors. And if not that, that we will at least recognize they are important pieces of the puzzle, gears that help keep nature running. Because as the conservationist Aldo Leopold once wrote about ecosystems: "To keep every cog and wheel is the first precaution of intelligent tinkering."

Check off any of the following animals that live in your community. Circle the animals you've seen or heard.

Birds

- ☐ pigeon
- ☐ house sparrow
- ☐ house finch
- ☐ mourning dove
- ☐ Canada goose
- ☐ seagull
- ☐ American crow
- ☐ American robin
- ☐ duck (species: _____)
- ☐ other: _____

Reptiles and Amphibians

- ☐ alligator
- ☐ frog (species: _____)
- ☐ toad (species: _____)
- ☐ turtle (species: _____)
- ☐ tortoise (species: _____)
- ☐ snake (species: _____)
- ☐ lizard (species: _____)
- ☐ salamander (species: _____)
- ☐ other: _____

Small Mammals

- ☐ chipmunk
- ☐ opossum
- ☐ armadillo
- ☐ raccoon
- ☐ skunk
- ☐ muskrat
- ☐ beaver
- ☐ squirrel (species: _____)
- ☐ rabbit (species: _____)
- ☐ bat (species: _____)
- ☐ otter (species: _____)
- ☐ other: _____

Large Mammals

- ☐ coyote
- ☐ black bear
- ☐ fox
- ☐ moose
- ☐ mountain lion
- ☐ deer (species: _____)
- ☐ sea lion (species: _____)
- ☐ seal (species: _____)
- ☐ other: _____

How do you respond when you see wildlife in the city?
Which word best describes your reaction to seeing wildlife in the city:
fear, annoyance, pity, respect, wonder, or curiosity?
Why do you think that is?

....
....
....
....
....
....
....
....
....
....
....
....
....
....
....
....
....
....
....

WEATHER TRACKER

Use the following chart to keep track of weather phenomena this month. First, create a key by coloring in the dots at the bottom of the page, using a different color for each circle. Then use this color-coded system to record each day's weather. Many days will have more than one type of weather.

SUNNY	CLOUDY	PARTLY CLOUDY	WINDY
○	○	○	○

RAINY	STORMY	SNOWY	FOGGY
○	○	○	○

WHERE THE WIND BLOWS

Spring has a reputation for being the windiest season. Most of the time, we don't think about wind unless it's destructive or a nuisance—damaging our property or simply blowing trash down the street. But this familiar phenomenon shapes our world in good ways, too. Wind shapes the land itself, and it moves things that can't move on their own, such as heat, cold, moisture, pollen, and seeds—all things that contribute to the flourishing of our planet.

Full Moon

Write down the date of this month's full moon and the time when it will rise so that you can observe it.

Date: _____   Time: _____

New Moon

Write down when the new moon occurs this month so you'll know the best time for stargazing.

Date: _____

Hydra, the Sea Serpent

Rippling through the sky like its namesake, the mythological sea serpent, Hydra is the largest of all constellations. In the northern hemisphere, Hydra is one of a few spring constellations that are visible only in January through May. See it now before it dips below the horizon. If you can't see stars where you live, you can learn their locations and see constellations virtually by using a website or app (see page 207 for suggestions).

In springtime, famous wildflower destinations such as California's deserts and Tennessee's mountains draw crowds of camera-toting tourists. But some of the best spring flowers are the ones that create beauty in places we don't expect to find it: the daffodils blooming in a ditch or the crab apple trees surrounding a traffic roundabout that burst into clouds of pink petals. Write down the spring blooms that surprise you this month and the unexpected places you see them.

Plant name or description	Date spotted	Place spotted

Birds aren't the only creatures that sing in spring. Warmer temperatures are a signal to frogs and toads to begin their short journeys to the ponds where they'll breed and raise their voices in an amphibian chorus. Frog and toad calls can be identified by species like bird calls can; it just takes some practice. As you watch for wildlife this month and fill out the chart below, consider learning about any frog or toad species common to your area.

Creature	Date spotted	Place spotted	Activity (if applicable)

SPRING GREENS

Spring is a popular time for foraging wild edible greens. Wild plants are typically the most tender and flavorful when they're young, which is why foragers often pick a plant's leaves, sprouts, or shoots when they first appear in spring. On page 35 are some spring greens that can be found throughout the US. Record any wild edibles you find or eat this month in the chart below (and remember to follow the guidelines on page 7 anytime you are foraging).

Plant	Where I discovered it	How I prepared it	Tasting notes

COMMON DANDELION (*TARAXACUM OFFICINALE*): The dandelion is a nutrient-rich plant disguised as a weed. This familiar plant grows nearly everywhere and is packed with vitamins A, C, and K, along with folate, potassium, and calcium. Furthermore, every part of a dandelion is edible, including its flowers, leaves, and roots.

OSTRICH FERN (*MATTEUCCIA STRUTHIOPTERIS*): The ostrich fern, like most ferns, can be found growing in shady, moist locations. In spring, the fern's sprouts emerge from the ground in tight green coils that resemble the ends of fiddles—which is why the sprouts are known as fiddleheads. Don't eat raw fiddleheads. Instead, you should sauté, roast, or pickle them.

WILD ASPARAGUS (*ASPARAGUS OFFICINALIS*): This plant looks and tastes like its garden-grown relative and grows wild in every state. Look for it in full sun near water sources or low areas that collect water, like ditches.

COMMON CHICKWEED (*STELLARIA MEDIA*): Chickweed is a common wild plant that spreads fast and grows in a mat along the ground. It has small leaves and small star-shaped white flowers. This plant is highly nutritious and can be eaten raw or even made into pesto as a substitute for basil.

FEED THE BIRDS

Nature is often closer than you think. But if you can't easily find nature, there are ways you can bring it to you. Chances are, wild birds live in your area (think of all the pigeons in the heart of big cities). If you want to see them, you may need to create the right conditions. Birds like places to perch (a balcony railing or windowsill will do), shelter or cover (like an awning or potted plant), and, most importantly, food.

To bring birds to you, install a birdfeeder on a patio or balcony, in the lawn, or attached to a window with suction cups. Not all bird species eat at feeders, but many songbirds do. And if you can't install a birdfeeder, you can attract birds with other types of food, like fruit on a windowsill. You can even adjust your offerings to attract the birds you most desire to see.

CRACKED CORN: cardinals, grosbeaks, jays, sparrows, pigeons, juncos

SUNFLOWER SEEDS: finches, chickadees, nuthatches, cardinals, woodpeckers

MILLET: doves, towhees, sparrows, wrens

THISTLE SEEDS: goldfinches, chickadees, juncos, pine siskins

RAISINS: bluebirds, mockingbirds, catbirds, robins, waxwings

ORANGE HALVES: orioles, bluebirds, scarlet tanagers, grosbeaks, woodpeckers

GRAPE JELLY: catbirds, orioles

If you fed birds this month, describe what you did—and the results—below:

....
....
....
....
....
....
....
....
....
....
....
....
....
....
....
....
....
....
....
....
....
....
....
....

notes from my natural habitat

Location: ....

Date & Time: ....

Weather & Temperature: ....

5 Things I See:

....

....

....

....

....

3 Things I Hear:

....

....

....

1 Thing I Smell:

....

1 Thing I Feel:

....

STOP AND SMELL THE OUTDOORS

Nature's scents can be as comforting as its sights and sounds. But when we spend our days in temperature-controlled homes and workplaces, we're cut off from the natural aromatherapy of the outdoors. This month, try practicing a mindfulness meditation that uses scent as its focus. Find a place outdoors where there are some pleasant natural scents or, if natural scents are in short supply, sit indoors near an essential oil diffuser. (Try pine, lavender, bergamot, eucalyptus, or wild orange essential oil.) Set a timer for three to five minutes. Then sit in a comfortable position and take three slow, deep breaths. Continue to breathe normally and focus on the scents until the timer sounds.

How do you feel afterward?
Did the scent remind you of anything?

....

....

....

....

....

....

....

....

....

....

Swallows

by Leonora Speyer

They dip their wings in the sunset,
They dash against the air
As if to break themselves upon its stillness:
In every movement, too swift to count,
Is a revelry of indecision,
A furtive delight in trees they do not desire
And in grasses that shall not know their weight.

They hover and lean toward the meadow
With little edged cries;
And then,
As if frightened at the earth's nearness,
They seek the high austerity of evening sky
And swirl into its depth.

Think about the ways you've experienced nature this month.
Pick an experience or something you observed and use it to
inspire your own poem below.

....

....

....

....

....

....

....

....

....

....

....

....

....

....

....

....

....

....

....

....

....

May

"If you look the right way, you can see that the whole world is a garden."

–Frances Hodgson Burnett

GROWING SEASON

I always have ambitious gardening dreams. When the ground thaws each spring, I want to sink my hands into the dirt and see what I can make. I imagine peonies, pink buds exploding into clouds of petals. I contemplate herbs: rosemary and thyme for bread and cocktail garnishes, and basil for pesto. I dream about roses, long lines of them. I research tomatoes, wishing I could find the strange and delicious heirloom variety I once bought at a farmers' market. Its rosy skin looked hand-painted, fine yellow brushstrokes tracing its curves. I wander my suburban garden center with a rattling shopping cart, making plans. Then I leave with a single rose bush and an armful of annuals and herbs. For now, my garden needs to fit on a balcony.

Every growing season is an experiment because I rarely plant the same thing twice. My gardening is informed by trial and error, and I research problems as they arise. This is how I learned about sawfly larvae and blossom-end rot and the shimmering metallic beetles that want nothing more than to chew straight through a newly opened rose. When I first spotted these insects, I marveled at their iridescence, glinting copper and emerald. Then I realized these jewel-like beetles are an invasive species that are difficult to thwart, and I revised my opinion of them.

I've watched videos on deadheading, and I've bought my first set of pruning shears, my only gardening tool. For everything else I use my hands, digging and weeding and plucking away the beetles and neon-green worms. I still wouldn't call myself a gardener, but I'm learning.

Maybe it's too easy for my generation to take plants for granted. Unlike our ancestors, most of us don't need to know which ones will harm us, heal us, or make a good salad. Maybe we're too busy for the slow work of sowing seeds in the dirt and nurturing the results. Or maybe some of us simply need a place to start, a kernel of curiosity that sprouts into something more.

For me, my botanical education began with two paperbacks, a field guide to native trees and another to regional wildflowers. The books taught me species names and how and where certain plants grow. But they also taught me to *see* the river birch and the white oak, the wild bergamot and the chicory. These books have turned plant strangers into neighbors. Now I pat the river birch's curled bark as I pass, and nod knowingly at the white oak near the pond and check it for acorns in the fall.

My field guides made me more curious about the world of plants. There are plenty of plant identification apps, of course, but I like the slow and tactile work of scanning an index and turning paper pages. And the books have the added advantage of *not* leading me down an internet rabbit hole where I end up shopping for pants when what I really want to do is identify the yellow flower at my feet.

Reading field guides and growing plants are both good ways to increase plant literacy, creating opportunities to deepen our knowledge about specific plants and the parts they play in our world. I never gave much thought to dahlias or tomato plants until I grew some myself. And I never knew which flowers attracted hummingbirds and bumblebees until I accidentally planted some of these creatures' favorites. Now I think about pollinators and about ways I can help the bees, butterflies, and birds that make plant life possible.

In one of his early memoirs, the environmental journalist Michael Pollan wrote, "The garden suggests there might be a place where we can meet nature halfway." I ponder this as I watch a hummingbird pass inches from my head and hover over the petunias, its wings thrumming like a guitar chord. My botanical contributions to the world are small, easy to miss among the suburban sprawl. But somehow, nature always seem to find my leafy gifts anyway. And every year, I watch and wait as we meet halfway.

WATER WORLDS

After the spring rains and before the summer heat, the world is green. Creeks run, ditches become ponds, and wetlands shimmer with water. While ecosystems like lakes and rivers usually exist year-round, some water worlds appear and disappear with the seasons. I grew up along the Mississippi River, and now I live in a city with several large lakes. But these days, the freshwater habitats I know best are the suburban retention ponds in my neighborhood. They're a habitat type that people are likely to overlook. These shallow, dredged ponds collect and store rainwater for our neighborhood. They're not much to look at, but after seeing these ponds in every season, I'm in awe of all the wild lives they support. Not only the plants that grow along their banks, but all the animals—birds, insects, fish, and amphibians—that depend on them for food and shelter.

Does your community have a well-known water habitat such as a lake, river, or even the ocean? What about lesser-known water worlds like retention ponds, drainage ditches, or even a park fountain or koi pond? Make a list below of any water habitats in your area, both the well-known and the overlooked. Visit a location or two from your list and journal about your experiences on the next page. While you're there, fill out this month's Flora and Fauna prompts too (see pages 50 and 51).

- ....
- ....
- ....
- ....
- ....

WEATHER TRACKER

Use the following chart to keep track of weather phenomena this month. First, create a key by coloring in the dots at the bottom of the page, using a different color for each circle. Then use this color-coded system to record each day's weather. Many days will have more than one type of weather.

SUNNY	CLOUDY	PARTLY CLOUDY	WINDY
○	○	○	○

RAINY	STORMY	SNOWY	FOGGY
○	○	○	○

CLOUD GAZING

Stargazing is a popular nighttime activity, but have you ever thought about watching the sky during the day? Just as you can read constellations to navigate, you can read the clouds to understand weather. Here is one type that is common this season:

Cumulonimbus

These large, tower-like clouds are possibly the most intimidating cloud type you'll see in the sky. Cumulonimbus clouds are also known as thunderheads because they can produce rain, hail, and lightning. (*Nimbus* is Latin for "rainstorm.") They're more common in spring and summer because of the unstable atmospheric conditions that can occur in these seasons. If you see cumulonimbus clouds forming, rain is likely on the way.

Full Moon

Write down the date of this month's full moon and the time when it will rise so that you can observe it.

Date: _____   Time: _____

New Moon

Write down when the new moon occurs this month so you'll know the best time for stargazing.

Date: _____

List or describe any plants you see during your visits to a water habitat.

Plant name or description	Date spotted	Place spotted

fauna

List or describe any animals, or wildlife signs, you see during your visits to a water habitat.

Creature/ wildlife sign	Date spotted	Place spotted	Activity (if applicable)

GROW A MICRO GARDEN

As much as I admire gardeners who raise row upon row of vegetables, fruits, herbs, and flowers, my limited outdoor space doesn't allow for this. But gardening doesn't have to be done on a large scale—or even outdoors—to be worthwhile. Flowers, root vegetables, and greens can all be successfully grown indoors or in very small spaces. If space and time restrict your gardening ambitions, consider these approaches:

- **Specialize.** Choose just one type of plant to grow, such as cherry tomatoes, basil, or petunias. One summer, I grew only two rose bushes on my balcony and learned all I could about caring for these high-maintenance plants.

- **Keep it small.** Another option is to grow a variety of things, but just one of each plant type, and limit the total number of plants to less than five.

- **Go low-maintenance.** Annuals (plants that last one growing season) can seem ordinary, but they're often hardy and self-sufficient. Plus, they're a great way to attract pollinators like butterflies and hummingbirds.

- **Start with seedlings.** You can shorten the time until harvest (or blooms) if you plant seedlings instead of seeds.

Use the chart on page 53 to plan your micro garden.

Plant species	When to plant	Where to plant	Sun or shade?	Watering needs	Date of bloom or harvest

Location: ....

Date & Time: ....

Weather & Temperature: ....

5 Things I See:

....

....

....

....

....

3 Things I Hear:

....

....

....

1 Thing I Smell:

....

1 Thing I Feel:

....

MOVE AT THE SPEED OF NATURE

Nature's pace is slower than ours. This month, try a mindfulness activity that invites you to move at a slower speed while using your senses. If possible, take a walk in your neighborhood or at a nearby park. Go alone or invite a friend to join you (but agree to at least a few minutes of silence). Silence your phone and avoid using earbuds or listening to anything else. Then walk at a leisurely pace, looking and listening to any bit of nature that's around you. When you slow down and put aside distractions, you might be surprised at what you see and hear.

What I Would Like to Grow in My Garden

by Katherine Riegel

Peonies, heavy and pink as '80s bridesmaid dresses
and scented just the same. Sweet pea,
because I like clashing smells and the car
I drove in college was named that: a pea-green
Datsun with a tendency to backfire.

Sugar snap peas, which I might as well
call memory bites for how they taste like
being fourteen and still mourning the horse farm
I had been uprooted from at ten.
Also: sage, mint, and thyme—the clocks
of summer—and watermelon and blue lobelia.

Lavender for the bees and because I hate
all fake lavender smells. Tomatoes to cut
and place on toasted bread for BLTs, with or without
the *b* and the *l*. I'd like, too, to plant
the sweet alyssum that smells like honey and peace,
and for it to bloom even when it's hot,

and also lilies, so I have something left
to look at when the rabbits come.
They always come. They are
always hungry. And I think I am done
protecting one sweet thing from another.

Think about the ways you've experienced nature this month.
Pick an experience or something you observed and use it to
inspire your own poem below.

June

"We all want quiet. We all want beauty . . . we all need space. Unless we have it, we cannot reach that sense of quiet in which whispers of better things come to us gently."

—Octavia Hill

NEARBY NATURE

A cemetery is a strange place for a picnic. But if you lived in an American city a couple of centuries ago, a cemetery was one of the rare places where you could sink your feet into lush grass or rest in the shade of a tree. In the nineteenth century, many urban cemeteries were popular destinations for people who wanted to escape to nature but didn't own land or a house with a yard.

Beginning with New York's Central Park in 1858, a landscape architect named Frederick Law Olmsted introduced a new type of green space to American cities: public parks that evoked the look and feel of the countryside, without tombstones. In Olmsted's vision, parks were designed to look scenic and a bit wild, rather than cultivated like the formal gardens found in European cities. Central Park became the inspiration for numerous parks across the US. Later, it was also Olmsted who first designed interconnected park systems within an urban area, or parkways: nature corridors along roads that linked one park to another.

City dwellers no longer depend on cemeteries for a dose of nature. Today, people have access to myriad public green spaces: city parks, county parks, state parks, open spaces, community gardens, schoolyards, nature preserves, and greenways. In a time when 80 percent of Americans live in cities or suburbs, public places where people can access nature are more important than ever, particularly because spending time outdoors is so good for us.

Among other benefits, we now know that time spent in nature lowers a person's cortisol levels (the stress hormone), improves the brain's ability to process information, and can reduce symptoms of depression, anxiety, and post-traumatic stress disorder. According to researchers in Finland, spending just five hours a month outside is enough to experience nature's positive effects on our minds and bodies. And those five hours can be accumulated gradually in short doses, including a bike ride or a backyard barbecue.

I don't think I understood the value of city parks until I moved into my current apartment. Its only outdoor space is a balcony off the living room. The balcony is not a quiet or restful place. It overlooks a parking lot that's busy with delivery trucks, trash collection, dog walkers, and cars. But one of the reasons my husband and I chose this apartment is because of what we can see beyond the hubbub: a city park.

At first glance, it's an unremarkable place. The park is a dandelion-flocked lawn that's several acres long, with rows of trees on two sides. A paved path runs through it, passing two ponds that are surrounded by cattails and wild parsnip. Since moving here several years ago, I've walked in this park nearly every day, no matter the season or weather. I've watched wildflowers bloom, foraged for black raspberries, collected fall leaves, and slid across the frozen ponds in my snow boots. But our park offers more than some natural scenery and a place to relax. This ordinary place is full of life.

Not long ago, I listed the animals I've seen or heard here and was shocked by the number. This small parcel, that's more cultivated than wild, provides habitat and food for more than forty animal species: animals like muskrats, great horned owls, coyotes, white-tailed deer, monarch butterflies, great blue herons, wild turkeys, painted turtles, kingfishers, hawks, sandhill cranes, and even a small sunfish species called a pumpkinseed.

And then of course, there are the human lives that rely on this place. The park is my neighborhood's public square, the one place where I regularly see my neighbors as they walk, jog, fish, picnic, and play fetch with their dogs. On summer days, this is where kids learn to ride bikes, people hang hammocks, and friends meet for picnics on the grass. On summer nights, this is where we linger after sunset, listening to the frogs and watching the fireflies drifting skyward like green sparks. It feels as if my neighbors and I belong to this place; that in some way, we're each a part of its ecosystem, shaping this small corner of nature as it shapes us.

Summer is the perfect time to explore nearby nature. Learn about the public green spaces in your community. Write their names and locations below and check off the ones you visit this season.

City parks:

- ☐ ....
- ☐ ....
- ☐ ....

County parks:

- ☐ ....
- ☐ ....
- ☐ ....

State parks:

- ☐ ....
- ☐ ....
- ☐ ....

Open spaces or other green spaces:

- ☐ ....
- ☐ ....
- ☐ ....

Gardens:

- ☐ ....
- ☐ ....
- ☐ ....

Greenways:

- ☐ ....
- ☐ ....
- ☐ ....

Nature preserves:

- ☐ ....
- ☐ ....
- ☐ ....

Describe what summer is like where you live—use your five senses and consider things like plants, wildlife behavior, daylight, weather, scents, colors, and how the season affects people.

....

....

....

....

....

....

....

....

....

....

WEATHER TRACKER

Use the following chart to keep track of weather phenomena this month. First, create a key by coloring in the dots at the bottom of the page, using a different color for each circle. Then use this color-coded system to record each day's weather. Many days will have more than one type of weather.

SUNNY	CLOUDY	PARTLY CLOUDY	WINDY
○	○	○	○

RAINY	STORMY	SNOWY	FOGGY
○	○	○	○

SUMMER SOLSTICE

On June 20 or 21, the Earth reaches its maximum tilt toward the sun, filling the northern hemisphere with light and warmth. In Scandinavia, the summer solstice—called midsummer—is celebrated widely and enthusiastically. This month, find your own way to celebrate the longest day of the year and the beginning of summer. Jot down an idea in the space below.

....

....

Full Moon

Write down the date of this month's full moon and the time when it will rise so that you can observe it.

Date: _____   Time: _____

New Moon

Write down when the new moon occurs this month so you'll know the best time for stargazing.

Date: _____

Jupiter

Jupiter is the oldest planet in our solar system, but it was only officially named by the scientific community in 1976. The planet's orange stripes are swirling gas clouds that can be seen with a telescope. To the unaided eye, Jupiter appears as a bright white star, and it is visible even in major cities.

Spring blooms have faded away and summertime plants have taken their place. In these early days of summer, what plants are blooming or producing fruit where you live? If you don't know their names, describe them in a few words.

Plant name or description	Date spotted	Place spotted

With warm weather and abundant food, summer is the time when most animals raise their young. The birds, mammals, and other creatures that were born in winter and spring are finally leaving their nests and dens to make their way into the world. Watch for young birds and other animals this month. Write down any young animals you see. If you can't identify the species (it's particularly hard with baby birds), describe them.

Creature	Date spotted	Place spotted	Activity (if applicable)

PICK-YOUR-OWN BERRIES

Early summer berries are a sign of a bigger harvest to come. This is the season for favorites such as strawberries and raspberries, but it's also the time when more obscure berries ripen in the wild. Berry-producing plants are hardy, and sometimes invasive, spreading quickly with or without human help. Record any wild berries (or other edibles) you find or eat this month in the chart below.

Berry or plant	Where I discovered it	How I prepared it	Tasting notes

If your local parks allow foraging, look for these plants; all three start to ripen in early summer.

BLACK RASPBERRY (*RUBUS OCCIDENTALIS*): Black raspberries grow in thickets along tree lines and in forested areas. They are much smaller than blackberries and have hollow centers like their cousins, the red raspberries.

JUNEBERRY (*AMELANCHIER*): Juneberry is known by several different names, including serviceberry, saskatoon, and shadbush. Each of these names actually refers to a group of about twenty species that share similar characteristics, and each produces edible berries. These plants can be either shrubs or small trees, and they produce sweet berries that can be red, purple, or black.

BLACK MULBERRY (*MORUS NIGRA*) AND RED MULBERRY (*MORUS RUBRA*): These trees produce similar berries (one black, the other red) that look like elongated raspberries. The red mulberry is native to North America.

SEEK OUTDOOR INSPIRATION

In architecture and interior design, *biophilic design* is a term for using nature as inspiration and creating harmony between indoor and outdoor spaces. But even if you're not a designer, using nature to decorate our homes has been shown to improve our mood and keeps us connected to the outdoors on days when work, illness, or other circumstances keep us inside. To bring more of the outdoors in, first think about the things in nature that bring you joy or peace. Do you love the shape of oak leaves, the color of a robin's egg, the smell of pine? Use the prompts below to record your answers.

Favorite places in nature:

- ....
- ....
- ....

Favorite colors in nature:

- ....
- ....
- ....

Favorite patterns in nature:

- ....
- ....
- ....

Favorite scents in nature:

- ....
- ....
- ....

Favorite sounds in nature:

- ....
- ....
- ....

Now brainstorm ways you can use these elements—favorite natural scents, colors, patterns, etc.—to inspire your home decor through paint colors, artwork, fabrics, scent diffusers, and found objects.

....

....

....

....

....

....

....

....

....

....

....

....

Location: ....

Date & Time: ....

Weather & Temperature: ....

5 Things I See:

....

....

....

....

....

3 Things I Hear:

....

....

....

1 Thing I Smell:

....

1 Thing I Feel:

....

GET IN THE FLOW

Whether it waves, rushes, rolls, or rains, the sound of water soothes the mind. That's because listening to water produces alpha waves in our brains, a natural electrical rhythm that's slow and calming. This month, find a place outdoors where you can listen to the sound of water for a few minutes, such as a river, lake, or park fountain. You can even sit by your window on a rainy day. If that's not possible, you can use a sound machine or app that plays water sounds for a similar benefit.

Where Innocent Bright-Eyed Daisies Are

by Christina Rossetti

Where innocent bright-eyed daisies are,
With blades of grass between,
Each daisy stands up like a star
Out of a sky of green.

Think about the ways you've experienced nature this month.
Pick an experience or something you observed and use it to
inspire your own poem below.

....

....

....

....

....

....

....

....

....

....

....

....

....

....

....

....

....

....

....

....

July

"Rest is not idleness, and to lie sometimes on the grass under trees on a summer's day, listening to the murmur of the water, or watching the clouds float across the sky, is by no means a waste of time."

–John Lubbock

WHEN NATURE IS UNCOMFORTABLE

Nature can be easier to love from a distance. Movies and social media tend to idealize outdoor experiences, blurring nature's harsher realities. People share photos of stunning vistas, but not their sunburns; dreamy forest campsites, but not the mosquitoes; inspiring quotes, but not the trailside argument they had with their hiking companions. As a person who writes about nature, I do it too. Nature is full of beauty, adventure, and goodness. I want to celebrate those parts of it. But if you spend enough time in the outdoors, you also discover that nature can be uncomfortable, unsettling, and sometimes scary.

I love nature. Most of the time, it leaves me quoting Mary Oliver and wishing I lived in a tree house. But not always. There have been plenty of times when nature has made me frustrated and fearful. I could tell you about the nights I've cowered in my tent as thunderstorms roared overhead. Or any number of hikes in the suburban wilds when it was too hot, too windy, or so muddy I could hardly walk uphill. I could also tell you about a kayak trip when I said something I never thought I'd say.

Just outside my city, there are several small rivers that flow nearly undetected. Each one appears as a blue squiggle on maps, but it's easy for people to overlook these little rivers as they wind through farm fields and sneak behind subdivisions. With twisting channels and dams of debris, they're best explored by kayak. One summer Saturday, my husband and I spent most of the day paddling one of these rivers. And not only paddling, but portaging.

Small rivers are frequently barricaded by fallen trees, and unless a volunteer comes through with a chainsaw, they stay that way. Hour after hour that day, we paddled until we reached an obstacle, hauled our kayaks up the mud-slicked banks, and dragged them through thornbushes until we reached open water again. Being in the water wasn't easier. The fast current and hidden boulders meant we had to be vigilant. I lost my sunglasses and nearly lost my paddle. Several times, I came close to capsizing, and my kayak was pinned against a submerged log by the powerful river more than once. Our "relaxing Saturday paddle" had stopped being a fun adventure shortly after it began.

By early evening, we checked our progress on our GPS app. That's when we learned that after all our exhausting work . . . we were just a third of the way to our destination. In a couple of hours, it would be dark, and the only thing more dangerous than paddling this river at all was paddling it at night. In that moment, nature taught me a new emotion: scared/angry. Our only option was to keep going. As we continued downriver, hauling our kayaks and fighting our way through thorns again, I said it out loud: "I hate nature." And in that moment, I meant it.

By the time we rounded the last bend in the river, the sun had set. My eyes had been slowly adjusting as the light grew dim and blue. Trees became jagged shadows. In the black water ahead, hazardous rocks became impossible to distinguish from harmless ripples. I floated along in the current, paddle poised, muscles tensed. Then I saw a small green spark. It was followed by another. Then another. Fireflies. The landing was up ahead now. I could hear my husband's kayak scrape the rocks as he pulled it out of the river. I wanted to ditch my boat and gratefully collapse on the shore, but the beauty of the blinking fireflies made me pause. I drifted in the dark, suspended between fear and wonder.

I don't believe people who say they dislike nature or the outdoors. Instead, I wonder if they haven't had the chance to experience the beautiful and the good along with the scary and the uncomfortable. Or maybe our collective idealization of nature does people a disservice. Maybe it'd be better if more people heard the message that nature is full of beauty *and* discomfort, fear *and* wonder. Most of the time, they go hand in hand. I have never forgotten that terrible kayaking trip. *And* I will always remember the fireflies.

Make a summer adventure list. What outdoor activities do you want to do this season? Do you want to watch a sunset, hike a trail, forage for wild berries, go stargazing, swim in a lake? List the activities below and check them off once you've done them. Write about one of your summer adventures on page 81.

☐ ....

☐ ....

☐ ....

☐ ....

☐ ....

☐ ....

☐ ....

☐ ....

☐ ....

☐ ....

☐ ....

☐ ....

☐ ....

☐ ....

☐ ....

☐ ....

WEATHER TRACKER

Use the following chart to keep track of weather phenomena this month. First, create a key by coloring in the dots at the bottom of the page, using a different color for each circle. Then use this color-coded system to record each day's weather. Many days will have more than one type of weather.

SUNNY	CLOUDY	PARTLY CLOUDY	WINDY
○	○	○	○

RAINY	STORMY	SNOWY	FOGGY
○	○	○	○

SUMMER CLOUDS

Cloud-watching is an easy outdoor activity you can do no matter the weather, location, or light pollution where you are. Here are two cloud types you might see this time of year.

Altocumulus

Dotting the sky like tufts of white wool, groups of altocumulus clouds can appear on humid summer mornings. Their presence can mean that thunderstorms are in the forecast.

Stratus

When the sky looks like a gray sheet or a thick fog hovers above the rooftops, you're looking at stratus clouds. *Stratus* means "layer" and this cloud type is flat and featureless, covering the whole sky. In summer, stratus clouds are common near coastlines, often giving way to sun by the afternoon.

Full Moon

Write down the date of this month's full moon and the time when it will rise so that you can observe it.

Date: _____ Time: _____

New Moon

Write down when the new moon occurs this month so you'll know the best time for stargazing.

Date: _____

The height of summer is a time of blooming and harvesting. Record any plants you see this month and note if they're blooming or producing fruit. You can even include locally grown plants—including fruit and vegetables—that you see at a summertime market in your area.

Plant name or description	Date spotted	Place spotted

Many plant species wouldn't exist without pollinators like insects and birds. What specific pollinators (insect, bird, or bat species) are native to where you live? Do some research or observe them in the wild. As you record the animals you see this month, include these helpful creatures too.

Creature	Date spotted	Place spotted	Activity (if applicable)

CREATE WITH NATURE

As you might remember from your school days, nature is full of craft supplies. But nature crafts aren't only for kids. Consider what you can make using the following natural materials. (In some places, collecting natural items is prohibited in order to protect ecosystems and prevent the spread of invasive species. Never collect any natural item without first knowing the property rules.)

DRIFTWOOD: coat hooks, wind chimes, picture frames, storage containers, shelves

WILD GRAPEVINE: wreaths, birdfeeders, baskets, garlands, wall hangings

ROCKS: doorstops, vase fillers, garden markers, drawer pulls, jewelry

PRESSED FLOWERS OR LEAVES: ornaments, bookmarks, greeting cards, wall art, jewelry

SHELLS: jewelry, vase fillers, drawer pulls, candle holders, trinket dishes

Record your scavenged items and your plans for them below.

notes from my natural habitat

Location: ....

Date & Time: ....

Weather & Temperature: ....

5 Things I See:

....

....

....

....

....

3 Things I Hear:

....

....

....

1 Thing I Smell:

....

1 Thing I Feel:

....

THINK LIKE A CLOUD

Clouds are often nearby, even when other forms of nature are more elusive. They're in constant, graceful motion above our heads, sometimes swirling past and sometimes drifting so slowly that they appear motionless. This month, turn a few moments of cloud-watching into a simple, mindful activity. First, wait for a day with clouds and go to a place outdoors where you can see some of the sky. You can stand, sit, lie down, or watch the sky however you feel comfortable. Choose one cloud and focus on it. Watch the cloud as it changes shape, builds up, or dissolves away. If you want, you can picture the cloud as one of your current worries to help visualize setting aside the worry for a while. Keep watching until you can no longer see the cloud or until it blends with other clouds.

Homeopathic

by Frank X Walker

The unripe cherry tomatoes, miniature red chili peppers
and small burst of sweet basil and sage in the urban garden
just outside the window on our third floor fire escape
might not yield more than seasoning for a single meal

or two, but it works wonders as a natural analgesic
and a way past the monotony of bricks and concrete,
the hum of the neighbor's TV, back to the secret garden
we planted on railroad property, when I was just a boy.

I peer into the window, searching for that look on mamma's face,
when she kicked off her shoes, dug her toes into dirt
teeming with corn, greens, potatoes, onions, cabbage, and beets;
bit into the flesh of a ripe tomato, then passed it down the row.

Enjoying our own fruit, we let the juice run down our chins,
leaving a trail of tiny seeds to harvest on hungry days like these.

Think about the ways you've experienced nature this month.
Pick an experience or something you observed and use it to
inspire your own poem below.

....
....
....
....
....
....
....
....
....
....
....
....
....
....
....
....
....
....
....
....

August

"Live in each season as it passes;
breathe the air, drink the drink,
taste the fruit, and resign yourself
to the influence of the earth."

–Henry David Thoreau

SMALL ACTS OF RESTORATION

The old barbed wire fence was an eyesore. It was also dangerous. Once upon a time it kept cows in a pasture, but now it was a hazard for hikers and wildlife (deer and owls are two species that can be fatally injured by such fences). The barbed wire dug its rusty claws into trees, coiled itself around shrubs, and hid in the underbrush. It would stay that way for decades unless someone removed it.

On a bright and windy morning, that was my assignment. I had joined a building project for the Ice Age Trail, a long-distance hiking trail that passes through my city as it traces the path of a long-ago glacier. Our group was prepping the land for a new trail segment. Most volunteers were uprooting invasive plants to restore the native forest. I decided to dismantle the barbed wire fence, a relic from when the land was a farm field.

I worked my way down the tree line with wire cutters, clipping the rusty fence, prying staples out of tree trunks, and gathering up the quivering wire as I went. It was slow work and a bit dangerous. Rusty barbed wire snags clothing and skin and swings wildly at your face when you cut it free. When I'd finished, I felt deep satisfaction. Now the trees and plants were unencumbered, and the deer, coyotes, and other animals could move freely, and safely, through the woods. It was one small act of restoration.

Wherever people live, trash follows. And in cities, more people means more trash. It's one of the most common ways we harm ecosystems. Some of it is accidental, some incidental, but plenty of garbage is intentional. I've watched people throw fast-food wrappers from car windows and heave their Christmas trees and Halloween pumpkins into ponds. In summer, grasses grow over soda cans and around disposable masks. Plastic cups fill with pond water, then mud, sinking to rest in the shallows. A vodka bottle, intact but empty, lies in the gutter among grass clippings. I live in one of the cleaner American cities, but still, trash persists. I've seen sheets of foam insulation cartwheeling through the neighborhood as the wind carries them from the same construction site, day after day. Later I'll see these sheets disintegrating into bits as they float in the local pond like fish eggs.

I don't know how to solve the larger environmental problems of our time. But I know how to pick up trash, so I do. It's one small act of restoration. When we notice more than the usual amount of litter, my husband and I grab a few trash bags and head outdoors. We untangle plastic bags from branches. We dig out bottle caps from the dirt. And we wade into pond muck to snag plastic bottles. Picking up trash is mundane. It doesn't feel like the work of a conservationist or environmental activist. It feels like cleaning up after a sloppy roommate. It feels futile. No matter how much trash we collect, there's always more.

Yet that doesn't mean my actions are meaningless. The problem is big, and I'll never solve all of it alone, but maybe I can make a difference for a few creatures, one microhabitat at a time. Picking up trash in my neighborhood means there's one less plastic bag that will harm the animals who live there. One less bottle cap that floats to the river and is swallowed by a hapless fish. And maybe for a week or two, my neighbors and I can enjoy the beauty of nature without having to overlook crumpled food wrappers and construction waste.

Caring for nature in ordinary, tangible ways like this can also change *us*. The botanist Robin Wall Kimmerer writes that "as we work to heal the earth, the earth heals us." I think that's true. Collecting litter, uprooting invasive plants, planting flowers, helping an injured animal–all these things change nature for the better. But they also do more than that. They help heal our relationship to nature itself, one small act of restoration at a time.

What are some actions you can take this month to help nature where you live? List them below:

- ....
- ....
- ....
- ....
- ....
- ....
- ....
- ....
- ....
- ....
- ....
- ....
- ....
- ....
- ....
- ....
- ....

Pick one or two of these ideas and set aside some time—
even five or ten minutes is enough—and do what you can.
Journal about your experiences below.

....

....

....

....

....

....

....

....

....

....

....

....

....

....

....

....

....

....

....

....

WEATHER TRACKER

Use the following chart to keep track of weather phenomena this month. First, create a key by coloring in the dots at the bottom of the page, using a different color for each circle. Then use this color-coded system to record each day's weather. Many days will have more than one type of weather.

SUNNY	CLOUDY	PARTLY CLOUDY	WINDY
○	○	○	○

RAINY	STORMY	SNOWY	FOGGY
○	○	○	○

STORMY WEATHER

Summertime is synonymous with storms. Storms can be ominous, and they can cause a lot of destruction. But not all storms do. Watching a thunderstorm roll in from a safe vantage point can be an awe-inspiring experience. There's something about a storm that reminds us we're a small part of something much larger. If the forecast works in your favor, take time to watch a storm this month.

Full Moon

Write down the date of this month's full moon and the time when it will rise so that you can observe it.

Date: _____ Time: _____

New Moon

Write down when the new moon occurs this month so you'll know the best time for stargazing.

Date: _____

Perseids Meteor Shower

In August, one of the most popular meteor showers lights up the sky: the legendary Perseids. Not only are these "shooting stars" among the flashiest and most numerous of the year, their peak coincides with ideal summertime stargazing conditions. Around mid-August, look toward the constellation Perseus to see the show.

Cities sizzle in summer. That's why city dwellers should plant more trees and protect the ones they have. Trees can lower the surrounding air temperature by five to ten degrees and create shade that's up to twenty degrees cooler than sunny areas nearby. Get to know the trees in *your* neighborhood. Where do they grow and what species are they? Record your findings in the chart below.

Tree species	Location	Observations

No matter where they grow, trees support many other living organisms. In fact, more than 80 percent of land animals live in forests. And in a city environment, a single tree can be an oasis for creatures like birds and squirrels. What are some animals that depend on trees where you live? Record any you see in the chart below.

Creature	Date spotted	Place spotted	Activity (if applicable)

notes from my natural habitat

Location: ....

Date & Time: ....

Weather & Temperature: ....

5 Things I See:

....

....

....

....

....

3 Things I Hear:

....

....

....

1 Thing I Smell:

....

1 Thing I Feel:

....

TREE THERAPY

Shinrin-yoku, or "forest bathing" as it's known in English, is a type of nature therapy that was first studied in Japan in the 1980s. It was developed as an antidote to burnout among Japanese workers but has since spread to other countries. The idea is straightforward: spend time in a forest or a place where you're among trees (even a tree-lined sidewalk will do) and your stress levels will fall. It doesn't really matter what you do: go for a walk or set up a hammock and relax. It's especially important to stow away your phone, camera, earbuds, or other devices. Not only will you experience fresh air and sunlight, trees release beneficial airborne chemicals called *phytoncides*, essential oils that have been shown to lower heart rates and blood pressure.

August

by Lizette Woodworth Reese

No wind, no bird. The river flames like brass.
On either side, smitten as with a spell
Of silence, brood the fields. In the deep grass,
Edging the dusty roads, lie as they fell
Handfuls of shriveled leaves from tree and bush.
But 'long the orchard fence and at the gate,
Thrusting their saffron torches through the hush,
Wild lilies blaze, and bees hum soon and late.
Rust-colored the tall straggling briar, not one
Rose left. The spider sets its loom up there
Close to the roots, and spins out in the sun
A silken web from twig to twig. The air
Is full of hot rank scents. Upon the hill
Drifts the noon's single cloud, white, glaring, still.

Think about the ways you've experienced nature this month.
Pick an experience or something you observed and use it to
inspire your own poem below.

September

"Autumn is the mellower season, and what we lose in flowers we more than gain in fruits."

–Samuel Butler

HIDDEN HARVEST

There isn't an orchard in Orchard Pointe. The old oaks were cut down in Oak Grove. And the only plant that grows in the Meadows is Kentucky bluegrass, cut sharp and short. It's ironic that our neighborhoods are often named for the natural features they uprooted. It's hard not to feel guilty when thinking about how housing developers demolished nature instead of collaborating with it. Sometimes, remnants of these older landscapes persist, stalwart survivors like oaks, apple trees, and wild roses. For much of the year, these relics blend anonymously into the background, but in fall, they reveal themselves, one ripe fruit at a time. They're part of the city's hidden harvest.

In September, small russet-red apples appear underfoot on my evening run, a little bruised from their drop to the sidewalk. If it wasn't for this telltale fruit, I'd never notice the wild apple trees tucked into the canopy. Most have grown so tall and long limbed it's difficult to pick them out from the surrounding maples. A wild apple looks like a commonplace fruit, but in another light, it's an artifact. Only three apple species are native to North America, all crab apples. That means the trees that drop the larger apples on my running route are a cultivated variety. Did someone plant the trees once upon a time? Are they a cultivar that's been lost to history? Foraged apples like these are imperfect. They're small, with the dents and scars that come from a feral upbringing. Many have bugs. But this doesn't mean they're worthless. Deer, squirrels, bears, foxes, raccoons, rabbits, and birds all eat wild apples.

Apples are only the most familiar of my city's hidden harvest. A closer look reveals much more: plums, grapes, rose hips, sumac berries, hickory nuts, acorns, and black walnuts. Not all of these plants are welcome in the neighborhood. Consider the black walnut. The black walnut tree, *Juglans nigra*, is native to North America and is legendary for its beautiful, tight-grained wood. It's also a pioneer species, among the first to grow in inhospitable places, leading some people to call it a "weed tree" despite its beauty and commercial value. In autumn, the tree yields walnuts, which is either very good or very bad depending on its location and your perspective.

North America's black walnuts have a similar flavor and nutritional value to English walnuts (the nonnative variety that's farmed in California and sold in grocery stores), but with notoriously tough shells, black walnuts are more difficult and costly to process. Fresh from the tree, black walnuts are surrounded by a thick green husk. They scatter across lawns like errant tennis balls, then decay into brown lumps. It's one reason homeowners often resent the trees. The other reason is that black walnut trees produce a chemical underground called *juglone* that kills some plant species that try to grow near it.

Some frustrated homeowners cut down these resilient trees. But at least one urban forager in my city has developed a solution that saves them. Each fall, he collects black walnuts (with permission) from yards throughout the city. Homeowners have the troublesome walnuts removed for free and the forager gets a free harvest he processes and sells to local restaurants and markets. Urban foraging like this has become a popular activity for city dwellers, and obliging neighbors with unwanted fruit are a good place to start. My sister-in-law harvests elderflowers and elderberries from a next-door neighbor who hadn't realized he owned the plant. One of my neighbors gives away their plums to passersby. When their tree's branches hang heavy with small, burgundy fruit, a chalk-scrawled note appears on the sidewalk with an arrow: *Free plums!* I happily fill my pockets.

I'm only a casual forager. I've never collected enough of anything to make a meal or put up stores for the winter. But my seasonal search can turn a stroll into a treasure hunt. And the taste of a foraged apple, tangy wild plum, or the maple-syrup sweetness of a hickory nut can still provide a sense of place, reminding me of the roots that grow alongside my own.

Research recipes that use ingredients (wild or cultivated) that are harvested in your community or region at this time of year. Is there a specific apple variety that's grown in your state? Do fall raspberries or squash show up at your farmers' markets this month? In the chart below, list any recipes you'd like to try that use locally harvested ingredients. Then take notes on the results! Record one or two of your favorite recipes on page 111.

Recipe name	Local ingredient	Tasting notes

WEATHER TRACKER

Use the following chart to keep track of weather phenomena this month. First, create a key by coloring in the dots at the bottom of the page, using a different color for each circle. Then use this color-coded system to record each day's weather. Many days will have more than one type of weather.

SUNNY	CLOUDY	PARTLY CLOUDY	WINDY
○	○	○	○

RAINY	STORMY	SNOWY	FOGGY
○	○	○	○

FALL EQUINOX

The fall equinox happens on or near September 20 each year. Twice a year on the spring and fall equinoxes, day and night are of nearly equal length.

The fall equinox has long been a time of celebration. Ancient civilizations built structures that perfectly aligned with the sun's position on the solstices or equinoxes, such as Stonehenge in England and Angkor Wat in Cambodia. But our modern world has its own serendipitous equivalents. For instance, "Chicagohenge" is an event that occurs on both the spring and autumn equinoxes. Chicago's downtown streets are designed as a grid that aligns with the points of the compass, so on the autumnal equinox, the sunrise and sunset align perfectly between a canyon of skyscrapers, filling the streets that run from east to west with beams of golden light.

This month, celebrate the fall equinox by watching the sunrise or sunset. Record the date and sunrise and sunset times of the fall equinox below.

Date: _____ Sunrise time: _____ Sunset time: _____

Full Moon

Write down the date of this month's full moon and the time when it will rise so that you can observe it.

Date: _____ Time: _____

New Moon

Write down when the new moon occurs this month so you'll know the best time for stargazing.

Date: _____

As summer and autumn overlap this month, some plants bloom for the first (or second) time while others are dropping their petals and fruit. Below, list some plants that are blooming or changing in other noticeable ways, such as changing colors, shedding leaves or fruit, or drying out.

Plant name or description	Date spotted	Place spotted

Autumn is a time of departures and arrivals in the animal world. Across North America, birds and some butterfly species are migrating from north to south. In the ocean, creatures such as whales and sea turtles are on the move too, and on land, mountain-dwelling animals move from high elevations to lower slopes and valleys. This month, watch the skies, land, and waters for migrating animals and record the species you see.

Creature	Date spotted	Place spotted	Activity (if applicable)

FALL FRUIT

No matter where you live, autumn offers fruit to forage. Harvest dates depend on plant species and location, with shorter, earlier harvests in northern regions and longer, later harvests in southern regions. If any of the following plants grow near you, look up their average harvest date in your area and write it down so you won't miss it. (See the Resources section on page 207 for recommended guides.)

STAGHORN SUMAC BERRIES: Staghorn sumac is a large shrub that gets its name from the way its crooked branches resemble antlers. In the fall, sumac leaves turn brilliant red and the plant produces cone-shaped clusters of dusty red berries. Fresh berries can be used to make a tart drink similar to lemonade, and crushed dried berries can be used as a spice rub.

Harvest date: _____

ROSE HIPS: All rose species produce small, round fruits that form after roses bloom. Apples and roses belong to the same family, so it's not surprising that rose hips look and taste like crab apples and are full of vitamin C. Fresh rose hips can be used to make jelly, sauce, or fruit leather, and dried rose hips can be used to make herbal tea.

Harvest date: _____

APPLES: Foraged apples that are sweet can be eaten raw, but if you pick tart and tangy crab apples, you may want to use them in a recipe. Wild apples of all types can be used to make applesauce, apple butter, or apple pie.

Harvest date: _____

GRAPES: There are many wild grape species that grow throughout the US, each of them ripening at slightly different times throughout late summer and fall. Like their wild apple counterparts, some wild grape species are very tart when eaten raw but can be used to make jam, juice, or even wine.

Harvest date: _____

Record any fruit (or other edibles) you find or eat this month in the chart below.

Fruit	Where I discovered it	How I prepared it	Tasting notes

PRESERVE FALL'S FLOWERS

Not all fall colors are in the treetops—you can also find them at your feet. September is a good time to gather fall-blooming wildflowers such as asters, goldenrod, and sunflowers. Like all wildflowers, these fall species often grow in unexpected places, like roadsides or empty lots. Preserve their beautiful blooms by taking a few photos. Then print the photos to share or display. Or take this journal and some colored pencils, and head outdoors to sketch fall blooms in the fresh air on the opposite page.

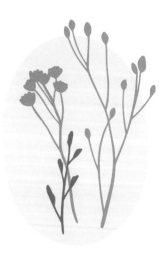

Location: ....

Date & Time: ....

Weather & Temperature: ....

5 Things I See:

....

....

....

....

....

3 Things I Hear:

....

....

....

1 Thing I Smell:

....

1 Thing I Feel:

....

SEE THE SEASON CHANGE

Watch autumn arrive, one leaf at a time. Choose a nearby tree that has leaves you can collect. Visit the tree every day for a week, collecting one leaf per day. Each time you select a leaf, take time to study it. Use your senses: feel the leaf's texture between your fingers, smell it, hold it up to the light. Whether or not you live in a place where leaves change color, notice how each leaf is different from the one you collected the previous day. At the end of the week, you can display or press the bouquet of leaves, if you wish.

Poem Beginning with a Line from It's the Great Pumpkin, Charlie Brown

by Maggie Smith

Just look—nothing but sincerity
as far as the eye can see—
the way the changed leaves,

flapping their yellow underbellies
in the wind, glitter. The tree
looks sequined wherever

the sun touches. Does anyone
not see it? Driving by a field
of spray-painted sheep, I think

the world is not all changed.
The air still ruffles wool
the way a mother's hand

busies itself lovingly in the hair
of her small boy. The sun
lifts itself up, grows heavy

treading there, then lets itself
off the hook. Just look at it
leaving—the sky a tigereye

banded five kinds of gold
and bronze—and the sequin tree
shaking its spangles like a girl

on the high school drill team,
nothing but sincerity. It glitters
whether we're looking or not.

Think about the ways you've experienced nature this month.
Pick an experience or something you observed and use it to
inspire your own poem below.

....
....
....
....
....
....
....
....
....
....
....
....
....
....
....
....
....
....
....
....
....

October

"Delicious autumn! My very soul is
wedded to it, and if I were a bird
I would fly about the earth seeking
the successive autumns."

–George Eliot

TINY FORESTS

All along my street, the leaves have brightened to gold and deepened to ruby. The honey locusts turned first, shimmering like sequins, and the maples followed. For many of us, trees are the overlooked backdrop of our lives, but in autumn, fleetingly, they command our attention. Most of us live near at least some trees. In fact, you might live near a forest and not even know it. That's because when we hear the word *forest*, we often think big and untamable: The rainforest. The boreal forest. Wild woodlands like these are so far removed from our everyday lives that they take on a mythical quality. We know they're crucial to the health of our planet, but we love them from a distance. In truth, we hardly know them.

The same could be said about our city forests: we hardly know them. And yet, unlike the trees of the wilderness, they're right in front of us. According to the US Forest Service, more than 140 million acres of America's forests are in cities and towns. The forest service defines *forest* generously, counting all the trees that grow in parks, river corridors, and boulevards—even solitary street trees planted along roadways. Whether we realize it or not, the city forest is all around, quietly doing the good work that trees do.

Trees add beauty to city life, softening the hard edges of a human-built world. On a philosophical level, trees can be our teachers, showing us what it means to grow and change, and demonstrating resilience. But the good work of city trees is tangible too. They make cities more livable for humans and wildlife alike, particularly in a changing climate. Like their wilder counterparts, city trees purify polluted air and capture carbon. They can cool the surrounding air by as much as ten degrees. And studies show that people who live near trees have lower blood pressure and lower levels of cortisol.

Given that they have so many known benefits, planting trees is a popular form of environmental activism. And it's not just single trees; there's a movement in Asian and European cities to plant small native forests in urban areas. These "tiny forests," as they're officially known, can be as small as two hundred square meters, a bit smaller than a tennis court. It's an innovative idea, but if you live in an American city, there's likely already a tiny forest near you. And it needs your protection.

Recently, three small forests in my neighborhood have been destroyed. The first forest was the most personal loss of the three. It covered less than two acres, but I could walk a few steps into it and forget I lived in the suburbs. Despite its small size, the forest was a complete ecosystem. It was a sanctuary for songbirds and a secret highway for white-tailed deer and a family of coyotes. I didn't know how old the forest was until I saw it in one of the first aerial photographs of the city; it had been there for nearly one hundred years.

Not long ago, a developer bought the forest and the adjoining field for a sprawling apartment complex. It never occurred to me that the trees were in danger because they were at the edge of the property. The forest's scenic value, if not its other benefits, seemed self-evident. Its destruction happened without warning. One afternoon I went for a walk and saw the forest had been clear-cut down to the dirt. Bulldozers were scooping its remains into piles. All those beautiful trees toppled and piled like kindling. A century-old forest community shredded into wood chips.

The story of my tiny suburban forest isn't unique. City trees throughout the US are being destroyed faster than they're being planted, at a rate of 175,000 acres a year. Too often, mature stands of trees are seen as obstacles to construction projects, and are replaced, if at all, by young saplings. But while it takes a few minutes to plant a tree, it takes years for that tree—and the ecosystem it creates—to reach its full potential. What our cities really need are not more tree planters, but tree stewards. Because we can save our city forests the same way we're demolishing them: by protecting one tree, one tiny forest at a time.

TRUE AUTUMN

Whereas September can be a shapeshifter, sometimes feeling like summer and fall in a single day, October is a month that's decidedly autumn. Flowers still bloom, but their blossoms are often upstaged by jewel-toned leaves. In the sky and seas, fall migration continues; and on land, animals and insects are making journeys and preparations of their own as the changing light, temperature, and something within tell them it's time.

All creatures have seasonal habits and rhythms.
Consider squirrels burying nuts to prepare for winter.
As you notice these things in nature, consider your own.
What are some seasonal habits and rhythms that connect
you to the autumn season?

....

....

....

....

....

....

....

....

....

....

....

....

....

....

....

....

....

....

WEATHER TRACKER

Use the following chart to keep track of weather phenomena this month. First, create a key by coloring in the dots at the bottom of the page, using a different color for each circle. Then use this color-coded system to record each day's weather. Many days will have more than one type of weather.

SUNNY   CLOUDY   PARTLY CLOUDY   WINDY
○   ○   ○   ○

RAINY   STORMY   SNOWY   FOGGY
○   ○   ○   ○

SHORT, COLORFUL DAYS

In late autumn, the sunrise dawdles and evenings lengthen. While diminishing daylight can be difficult for people, there are things in nature that depend on it. Fall colors, for instance. For many trees, shorter days signal that it's time to store nutrients for winter. The green pigment in their leaves, chlorophyll, breaks down, and the tree reabsorbs the nutrients into its twigs. With the chlorophyll gone, other pigments in the leaves like orange and yellow are revealed. The next time you marvel at fall colors, think about how shorter days and less light are catalysts, revealing the hidden beauty of the leaves. Below, record a few benefits that shorter days could have in your own life.

....

....

....

....

Full Moon

Write down the date of this month's full moon and the time when it will rise so that you can observe it.

Date: _____   Time: _____

New Moon

Write down when the new moon occurs this month so you'll know the best time for stargazing.

Date: _____

Fall color destination usually refers to a place that is famous for its stunning autumn trees. People will travel miles to see an aspen grove in full glow or a panorama of sugar maples. Yet we don't have to travel far to see autumn's beauty; it's waiting in places like highway medians, mall parking lots, and city parks. Note where you see beautiful trees and plants this month, especially ordinary places.

Plant name or description	Date spotted	Place spotted

Not all animals are on the move in the fall. Some are preparing to stay put by digging burrows, building lodges, eating, or storing food. When you're outside this month, note any changes in wildlife behavior.

Creature	Date spotted	Place spotted	Activity (if applicable)

COLLECT COLOR

Autumn leaves fade quickly, but you can prolong their beauty by pressing them. No special tools are necessary. Collect some colorful leaves that haven't dried out yet. Then flatten them between two pieces of waxed paper and tuck them underneath or within a heavy book. It'll take about two weeks for the leaves to fully dry, but when they do, they'll still have some of their color. Even if leaves don't change where you live, you can still press leaves or flowers as mementos of the season. Paste or sketch your pressings on the opposite page.

Location: ....

Date & Time: ....

Weather & Temperature: ....

5 Things I See:

....

....

....

....

....

3 Things I Hear:

....

....

....

1 Thing I Smell:

....

1 Thing I Feel:

....

LISTEN TO NATURE'S SOUNDTRACK— AND EVERYTHING ELSE

In a city, nature's sounds are mixed with human-made ones such as car engines, planes, and people talking, laughing, or shouting. It can be easy to miss the natural sounds *and* tempting to see the human-made noises as unwelcome intrusions. A type of mindfulness meditation called *sound meditation* offers a remedy for both tendencies. Sit in a comfortable position either outdoors or near an open window. Set a timer for three to five minutes, then close your eyes. For those few minutes, actively listen for any and every sound instead of trying to ignore or block them out. You may be surprised at what you hear or how your reaction to certain sounds changes or softens.

October

by Helen Hunt Jackson

Bending above the spicy woods which blaze,
Arch skies so blue they flash, and hold the sun
Immeasurably far; the waters run
Too slow, so freighted are the river-ways
With gold of elms and birches from the maze
Of forests. Chestnuts, clicking one by one,
Escape from satin burs; her fringes done,
The gentian spreads them out in sunny days,
And, like late revelers at dawn, the chance
Of one sweet, mad, last hour, all things assail,
And conquering, flush and spin; while, to enhance
The spell, by sunset door, wrapped in a veil
Of red and purple mists, the summer, pale,
Steals back alone for one more song and dance.

Think about the ways you've experienced nature this month.
Pick an experience or something you observed and use it to
inspire your own poem below.

....

....

....

....

....

....

....

....

....

....

....

....

....

....

....

....

....

....

....

....

....

November

"Outdoors we are confronted
   everywhere with wonders;
   we see that the miraculous is not
   extraordinary, but the common mode
   of existence. It is our daily bread."

                                        –Wendell Berry

ENDINGS AND BEGINNINGS

A raucous wind scatters the loose leaves and sends a chill through the air. Frost is in the forecast again, so I toss some worn beach towels over the plants on our balcony. There's no reason to save them. My negligence has already turned my pot of thyme into *dried* thyme, and the dahlias and petunias have become lethargic in their blooming. But I'm not ready to let them go. Or maybe it's the season I'm not ready to release: the season of plants growing outdoors; the ability to look out the window and see life, its leaves reaching open-handed to the sunlight.

November has a melancholy reputation. Where I live, it's an in-between time when the last leaves have fallen but the first snows have not. Nature's bold autumn palette has faded. Plants have shriveled, and animals have burrowed into the earth. In other words, late autumn isn't known for being a season of life and rebirth. That reputation belongs to spring, with all its new growth bursting from the ground and buds yawning awake. Spring is nature's trumpet call announcing the new, while late autumn is more like a lullaby played by a quiet violin. But these subdued days at the end of the year have a beautiful secret: *this* is when new life begins.

People love flowers, especially when they create a spectacle. A nearby county park once had a reputation for its sunflowers. In late summer, the sloped fields were full of the bright, gangly flowers packed shoulder to shoulder. The sunflowers attracted more than 100,000 people, nearly half my city's population. For days, cars clogged the parking lots and nearby streets, and crowds shuffled along the park's paths as if on a pilgrimage.

This clamoring to capture the fleeting beauty of flowers is repeated in other places—California's famed poppy fields come to mind. I understand the impulse. But I also think we would do well to remember the origins of all that beauty and wonder. Because like so many things in life, they have humble beginnings in a season we're likely to overlook. If you love spring, summer, and flower selfies, you have the subdued days of late autumn to thank, the time when nature casts its final seeds and the seeds go to work.

Seeds are as diverse as the plants they sprout. Large and small, spiky and smooth. They can be as impenetrable as stones or as delicate as tissue paper. Some float through the air on feathery parasols or papery wings. Others stay hidden inside fruit, tempting birds and squirrels to take them farther afield even as the ground freezes. Many seeds don't merely survive the harsh winter weather, they need it. Unlike hibernating animals, who doze in the dark until warmer temperatures wake them up, the seeds in my part of the world don't sleep or idly wait until spring.

The colder, darker days of the year are a time of preparation for some seeds. Their dormancy is broken *not* by a rise in temperature but by a drop, starting a process called cold stratification. The seeds of apples, wild roses, milkweed, and perennial wildflowers, along with acorns, have tough shells that protect them from sprouting too early. These shells must be broken down over time by freezing, thawing, and absorbing the moisture that comes through frost, rain, or snow. It can take up to several months, depending on the seed and the weather. But whenever spring comes, the seed must be ready to shrug off its time-worn coat and grow.

Seeds can be easier to spot during the in-between time. In November, I head to the park, the early sunset catching me by surprise. A few asters are still blooming, purple splashes in a beige sea. But I'm here for the seeds. A nearby tree shakes off a walnut with a thud. The last of the cattails have burst, revealing their woolly seeds. And a few tufts of milkweed seeds cling to dried stalks. A breeze tugs at the milkweed, pulling a few downy seeds loose. As I watch them float upward, I wonder about their eventual destinations. And despite the evening chill, I think about how, appearances to the contrary, nature's growing season always ends with a beginning.

A CHANGE OF PERSPECTIVE

After autumn's vivid colors and leafy confetti, November–with its hints of winter–can seem staid and subdued. Everything outdoors feels a bit too bare, even exposed. But this lack of flowers and foliage can also bring about discoveries: the seeds of next spring and signs of hidden wildlife. It can also lead to a new way of looking at a landscape, revealing contours and shapes you didn't notice before.

Andrew Wyeth, a painter known for his realism and landscapes, once said: "I prefer winter and fall, when you can feel the bone structure in the landscape." Think about this quote the next time you go outside. How do this month's seasonal changes offer a new perspective on familiar outdoor views and landscapes? Record your thoughts on page 145.

WEATHER TRACKER

Use the following chart to keep track of weather phenomena this month. First, create a key by coloring in the dots at the bottom of the page, using a different color for each circle. Then use this color-coded system to record each day's weather. Many days will have more than one type of weather.

SUNNY	CLOUDY	PARTLY CLOUDY	WINDY
○	○	○	○

RAINY	STORMY	SNOWY	FOGGY
○	○	○	○

WHEN IT RAINS

Winter doesn't officially begin until December, but nature doesn't heed our calendars or clocks. Winter weather like rain, sleet, or snow can occur in November, if not sooner. Although weather varies from region to region, increased cloudiness and precipitation is more common during this season in most places. And fittingly, the English word *winter* is likely related to the Old English or Old German words for "wet" or "water." Do you dread rain and snow, or welcome the coziness it can inspire? Record your thoughts below.

....

....

....

....

....

....

Full Moon

Write down the date of this month's full moon and the time when it will rise so that you can observe it.

Date: _____   Time: _____

New Moon

Write down when the new moon occurs this month so you'll know the best time for stargazing.

Date: _____

Although fall is harvest season in the northern hemisphere, for many trees and plants it's also time to sow as they finally release their seeds. Choose a plant or tree species near you that releases seeds in the fall and learn about it. Record what you learn below.

Plant/tree name: ....

Type of seed: ....

What disperses the seed (wind, birds, etc.): ....

Germination time: ....

Conditions needed for germination: ....

When do the seeds sprout? ....

Sketch the seed and plant in the space below:

As November pulls the curtain aside, signs of hidden wildlife abound: bird nests and squirrel dreys along with burrow entrances, deer beds, shelled nuts, feathers, eggshells, and animal tracks. Use the chart below to record any wildlife signs you see this month. Pay particular attention to things that were previously hidden in warmer, leafier seasons.

Creature/ wildlife sign	Date spotted	Place spotted	Activity (if applicable)

CHANGE YOUR SCENERY

Nature has a peculiar power that scientists are slowly beginning to understand. It's not only the scents and sounds of the outdoors that can heal, calm, and restore our bodies and minds. Sometimes the mere sight of nature is enough. Of course it'd be wonderful if everyone had a scenic view from their homes—the ocean, a mountain range, even a sturdy tree thick with leaves—but for many of us, that's not the case. A simple solution seems almost too good to be true: hang a photo of nature somewhere in your home where you can regularly see it. It sounds strange, but research shows that staring at a nature photo—for less than a minute!—can calm our minds and increase our focus. On the following page, paste a copy of your chosen photo, or if you'd prefer, sketch a favorite landscape.

notes from my natural habitat

Location: ....

Date & Time: ....

Weather & Temperature: ....

5 Things I See:

....

....

....

....

....

3 Things I Hear:

....

....

....

1 Thing I Smell:

....

1 Thing I Feel:

....

CONNECT TO THE EARTH

Try a mindfulness meditation inspired by trees. One of the reasons deciduous trees shed their leaves each year is to protect them from harsh winter weather like wind, snow, and ice that could weigh down and break their branches. In the coming season, a tree's intricate and flexible branches will be easy to see. Likewise, trees have branch-like root systems, anchoring themselves deep into the earth. Sit or stand in a comfortable position and set a timer for two to three minutes. (Close your eyes if it helps you focus.) For these few minutes, think like a tree, and imagine being securely grounded in the earth with deep roots while staying flexible in the midst of changing circumstances.

Fall, Leaves, Fall

by Emily Brontë

Fall, leaves, fall; die, flowers, away;
Lengthen night and shorten day;
Every leaf speaks bliss to me,
Fluttering from the autumn tree.
I shall smile when wreaths of snow
Blossom where the rose should grow;
I shall sing when night's decay
Ushers in a drearier day.

Think about the ways you've experienced nature this month.
Pick an experience or something you observed and use it to
inspire your own poem below.

....

....

....

....

....

....

....

....

....

....

....

....

....

....

....

....

....

....

....

December

"As children, we are very sensitive to nature's beauty, finding miracles and interesting things everywhere. As we grow up, we tend to forget how beautiful and magnificent the world is. There is magic and wonder for eyes who know how to look with curiosity and love."

–Ansel Adams

EVERYDAY WONDER

The brightness of the wintry world made me blink when I first pulled aside the curtains. Before my thoughts could fixate on my ice-covered windshield and slippery morning commute, I stood transfixed at the window. The snow had changed everything. It was as if someone had dropped a bag of sugar from a great height, turning the parked cars into soft mounds and coating every branch and balcony railing with a glistening layer of white. All was quiet. A strange but comforting hush had fallen along with the snow.

Snow reminds me that my inner child is alive and well. Maybe not late winter snow when I'm yearning to see the first hints of green underfoot, but the first snowfall of the season always stirs up a sense of wonder I thought I'd lost. Nature has a way of doing that. Throughout history, the beauty and mystery of nature has had a powerful pull on the human heart. Sometimes it moves people to write poems, create art, or try to capture it with photos. Sometimes it compels people to dig deeply into biology, ecology, and other assorted "-ologies" to better understand its inner workings. And sometimes, when faced with nature's magnificence, all we can do is stand in its presence. We feel small, not like a speck of dust but small like "the tiniest nail in the house of the universe," as the poet Mary Oliver writes.

The word for this reaction is *awe*. Awe is a powerful but barely studied emotion. Some psychologists refer to it as a "power emotion" because of its profound influence on our behavior and well-being. Awe can be defined as a mixture of dread, veneration, and wonder. Paul Piff, a social psychologist at the University of California, Irvine, simplifies it further: "awe is something that blows your mind." And once it sprouts, awe blooms into other positive emotions like joy, contentment, and gratitude. There's even a connection between awe and altruism. Several years ago, Piff and his colleagues conducted a research study about this very topic. They discovered that when people experience a sense of awe, they're more likely to, in academic-speak, "engage in pro-social behavior." What that means is that awe has the power to shift our focus from ourselves to others. It makes us more likely to consider the common good and leads us to actions like helping other people and being generous with our money and time.

Nature has a unique ability to awaken awe in us—whether it's a mountain, sunset, or unexpected snowfall. And in the past few years, researchers have gathered the data to support this too. Other things in life, like success at work or good friendships, can create a sense of joy or gratitude, but very few things ignite awe the way nature does. And while this emotion can lead to a more profound selflessness, awe can also heal our wounds. For instance, at the University of California, Berkeley, researchers have found that experiencing awe in nature—in this case, river-rafting trips in the wilderness—can help heal military veterans and at-risk youth who are dealing with PTSD and other types of trauma.

But wilderness adventure isn't the only way to experience awe in nature, of course. The world around us offers natural wonders large and small—from the sun setting behind a city skyline to tree limbs bending like dancers in the wind. In my own life, the changing seasons are a source of awe: spring's new life, summer's storms, autumn's changing leaves, and winter's snow. Despite a lifetime of winters, I still feel childlike wonder the morning after the first snowfall. And I think of the words of the British novelist J. B. Priestly, who wrote, "The first fall of snow is not only an event, it is a magical event. You go to bed in one kind of a world and wake up in another quite different, and if this is not enchantment then where is it to be found?"

Describe what winter is like where you live. Use your senses and consider things like plants, wildlife behavior, daylight, weather, scents, colors, and how the season affects people.

....

....

....

....

....

....

....

....

....

....

....

....

....

....

....

....

....

....

....

....

....

Reflect on the Ansel Adams quote that appears at the beginning of this chapter. List some things in nature that give you a sense of wonder or awe—try to think like a child again if that helps. Then add to the list throughout the month. Be on the lookout for wonder.

- ....
- ....
- ....
- ....
- ....
- ....
- ....
- ....
- ....
- ....
- ....
- ....
- ....
- ....
- ....
- ....
- ....
- ....

WEATHER TRACKER

Use the following chart to keep track of weather phenomena this month. First, create a key by coloring in the dots at the bottom of the page, using a different color for each circle. Then use this color-coded system to record each day's weather. Many days will have more than one type of weather.

SUNNY	CLOUDY	PARTLY CLOUDY	WINDY
◯	◯	◯	◯

RAINY	STORMY	SNOWY	FOGGY
◯	◯	◯	◯

WINTER SOLSTICE

The winter solstice marks the shortest day and longest night in the northern hemisphere. Around December 20 each year, the top of the planet begins to tilt once again toward the sun. The lands near the Arctic Circle have been in complete darkness for months by this time, but in the weeks after the winter solstice, the sun will finally send its first rays over the horizon again. People who live in northern Greenland have a community tradition of greeting the return of the sun together with song. Inspired by the people of Greenland, consider how you might commemorate the return of the light in your own way. Jot down an idea below.

....

....

....

....

Full Moon

Write down the date of this month's full moon and the time when it will rise so that you can observe it.

Date: _____   Time: _____

New Moon

Write down when the new moon occurs this month so you'll know the best time for stargazing.

Date: _____

Long before the Christmas tree tradition was brought to North America, evergreens were a wintertime symbol of life. And while conifers (trees with cones) such as firs, pines, and spruces are the most ubiquitous evergreens this time of year, they're not the only trees that stay green in all seasons. Arborvitae, boxwood, cedar, cypress, hemlock, rhododendron, and sequoia are all evergreens too. Do you notice any evergreen trees or shrubs where you live? Record them below.

Plant name or description	Date spotted	Place spotted

Not every creature comes and goes with the changing seasons; some stay right where they are and adapt, including squirrels, muskrats, coyotes, blue jays, and cardinals. What are some local animal species that are present year-round where you live? Record them below.

Creature	Date spotted	Place spotted	Activity (if applicable)

A SENSE OF PLACE

You don't have to head outside with a forager's bag–or wait until spring–to eat food from your local ecosystem. With farm-to-table restaurants, farmers' markets, community gardens, and a rise in urban agriculture, it's getting easier to eat locally in all seasons, even if you live in a city.

This month, try some foods grown or produced in your own community and think about their terroir. *Terroir* is a French word that means "sense of a place." First used as a winemaking term, it refers to the combination of environmental factors (soil, sunlight, etc.) that give a food its unique character and flavor. In addition to fresh produce (which might be in short supply this month where you live), try one of these local products.

HONEY: Honey made by your local bees is also made from local plants. The differences may be subtle, but honey from where you live will taste different from mass-produced honey because the bees use pollen from flowers in your area.

JAMS AND PRESERVES: If you don't have the capacity to garden, go to a farmers' market to find jams and preserves made from the local harvest.

DRIED HERBS OR HERBAL TEAS: Herbs gathered during the growing season can be dried and used as seasonings or combined with other botanicals to make herbal infusions (commonly known as herbal teas, although they contain no tea).

CHEESE: Cheese is a food that is made year-round, but artisan cheesemakers often have seasonal flavors and varieties that are made especially for winter recipes and holidays.

Use the chart below to keep track of local growers and producers you like. Continue using this chart in other seasons, too.

Business name	Food products sold	Where they sell

FORAGE FOR WINTER DECOR

The holiday season is one of the rare times when it's common to decorate by bringing the outdoors in. If you buy a real evergreen tree for the holidays, you can cut off some of the lower or inner branches and use them as decoration. If the branches are trimmed off at the tree lot, ask to take them with you. Or head outdoors on a seasonal scavenger hunt for natural items. (In some places, collecting natural items is prohibited in order to protect ecosystems and prevent the spread of invasive species. Never collect any natural item without first knowing the property rules.)

EVERGREEN BRANCHES: Garlands, wreaths, bouquets

PINE CONES: Garlands, vase filler, gift toppers, hanging ornaments

ACORNS: Vase fillers, hanging ornaments

GRAPEVINE: Wreaths, hanging balls, topiary frames

TWIGS: Bouquets, lighted twig "trees"

WINTERBERRIES: Bouquets, gift toppers

Record your scavenged items and your plans for them below.

Location: ....

Date & Time: ....

Weather & Temperature: ....

5 Things I See:

....

....

....

....

....

3 Things I Hear:

....

....

....

1 Thing I Smell:

....

1 Thing I Feel:

....

GO SOLO

The outside world can be quieter in winter. The absence of nature's sounds and other people *can* make the outdoors feel a bit lonely. But at the same time, this season of relative quiet is the perfect time to seek solitude. If you're able, spend some time outdoors alone this month. Consider taking a walk, visiting a park, or sitting outside for a few minutes. Dress warmly if necessary, bring a hot drink, keep your phone screen out of sight, and let your mind wander. Quiet might be better company than you think.

Winter Branches

by Margaret Widdemer

When winter-time grows weary, I lift my eyes on high
And see the black trees standing, stripped clear against the sky;

They stand there very silent, with the cold flushed sky behind,
The little twigs flare beautiful and restful and kind;

Clear-cut and certain they rise, with summer past,
For all that trees can ever learn they know now, at last;

Slim and black and wonderful, with all unrest gone by,
The stripped tree-boughs comfort me, drawn clear against the sky.

Think about the ways you've experienced nature this month.
Pick an experience or something you observed and use it to
inspire your own poem below.

....

....

....

....

....

....

....

....

....

....

....

....

....

....

....

....

....

....

....

....

January

"Sunshine is delicious, rain is refreshing, wind braces us up, snow is exhilarating; there is really no such thing as bad weather, only different kinds of good weather."

—John Ruskin

WINTER INTERLUDE

Winter can be bleak in a city. Snow helps—enough to frost the rooftops and withered lawns, a crumb coat on an imperfect cake. But even in the upper Midwest where I live, snowfall is unreliable. And without fresh snow, January can be especially dreary, the landscape shades of gray. The trees are skeletal. And the music of the birds is gone. Now the only sounds I hear outdoors are human-made: the distant hum of traffic, slamming car doors, a siren.

Writers have not been kind to winter. In everything from fairy tales to survival stories to dour Victorian poetry, winter is a metaphor for death and grief. I get it. I've always lived in a place where winter is a time of darkness, ice, and air so cold it hurts to breathe. And while there are things in nature that die with winter's arrival, it isn't only a season of death and decay. Nearly everywhere, winter is an interlude, a pause that can last a few notes or an entire movement. Our world wouldn't be the same without it.

Most of us know that sleep is necessary for our well-being. But you may not know that sleep's overarching purpose is restoration. When we drift off to sleep each night, our body begins housekeeping. Cell waste is rinsed away from our brains, clearing our minds. Short-term memories are collected and filed in long-term storage. Tissues, muscles, and joints are repaired by the release of a growth hormone. Our heart and lungs can rest as everything within us slows down. Without sleep, none of this invisible inner maintenance could happen.

Nature needs sleep and restoration too. The natural world follows a longer cycle of activity and rest dictated by the seasons. Our fellow animals sleep and hibernate, but so do trees and other plants. Among plants, the technical name for this rest is *dormancy* (from the Latin verb for sleep, *dormire*). Deciduous trees shed their leaves and enter dormancy to become aerodynamic and flexible in the face of winter's wind, snow, and ice. Even trees in warm climates, such as palms, can experience annual rest.

Like sleep for us, dormancy gives plants a much-needed break. The frenetic activity of spring, summer, and fall is exhausting. It takes a lot of energy for plants to process nutrients, grow, reproduce, and defend themselves against pests and disease. Many trees would eventually work themselves to death without winter's merciful interlude. Studies have shown that when a deciduous tree like a maple is kept indoors with constant warmth and light, it will skip dormancy during the first winter it spends indoors, but will subsequently die within a year or two. It needs winter, as we need rest.

The fallow January world reminds me that in nature there's no such thing as constant growth and activity. The visual cues of the bare trees, the muted colors, and the stillness remind me of my own need for restoration. In a way, the sleeping natural world gives me permission to slow the pace of my own life and accept that dormancy is part of a healthy life cycle.

Even so, it's hard to be awake when nature is asleep. For humans, hibernation (i.e., staying indoors until spring) is tempting. I know people who avoid the outdoors altogether in winter; they give up biking, hiking, even walking the dog to the corner and back. And although hibernation is fine for some mammals, it's not good for us. We're better off with regular doses of fresh air, daylight, and the sights and sounds of the outdoors.

It helps to think more like chickadees. Instead of fleeing cold winters like so many of their avian cousins, these indomitable little birds adapt to the season by caching food, sleeping at night in tiny holes made by woodpeckers, and even lowering their body temperatures in a type of controlled hypothermia. One thing that doesn't change with the seasons, though, is the chickadee's spiritedness. I'm still surprised when I hear their impossibly cheerful calls during swirling snowstorms and on winter's coldest mornings. It's a sound that coaxes me outdoors, reminding me that even though nature looks and feels different right now, I can find ways to adapt and thrive too.

A WORLD AT REST

While we're ringing in the new year, nature is resting. For animals, plants, and even soils, the quiet weeks of midwinter can be a much-needed pause. Sometimes the stillness and emptiness of the outdoors this time of year—human-made noises aside—can be unnerving. Even the ever-present gray squirrels, who don't truly hibernate, make themselves scarce. Yet rest is a normal stage in many life cycles. Sometimes, we might do well to follow nature's lead.

Consider dormancy in the natural world. In what ways do *you* need rest before launching into another year? What might that look like this month?

WEATHER TRACKER

Use the following chart to keep track of weather phenomena this month. First, create a key by coloring in the dots at the bottom of the page, using a different color for each circle. Then use this color-coded system to record each day's weather. Many days will have more than one type of weather.

SUNNY	CLOUDY	PARTLY CLOUDY	WINDY
○	○	○	○

RAINY	STORMY	SNOWY	FOGGY
○	○	○	○

ICE RAINBOWS

Rainbows are a common sight in spring and summer, arcing across the sky after a storm. But a special type of rainbow is more frequently seen in winter: a sun dog. Sun dogs are bright patches of light (sometimes rainbow-colored) that appear on one or both sides of the sun. They're also called *mock suns*. Rainbows appear when sunlight passes through raindrops, but sun dogs occur when sunlight passes through thin clouds of ice crystals. Sometimes a sun dog will even form a rainbow-colored halo around the sun.

Full Moon

Write down the date of this month's full moon and the time when it will rise so that you can observe it.

Date: _____   Time: _____

New Moon

Write down when the new moon occurs this month so you'll know the best time for stargazing.

Date: _____

Ursa Major, the Great Bear

The Big Dipper is one of the most recognizable star patterns in the sky. It's visible all year and has an easy-to-spot shape: a four-cornered ladle with a bent handle. The Big Dipper is part of a larger constellation called Ursa Major, or the Great Bear. The ladle forms the back half of the bear and the handle is the bear's tail.

Choose a few plants that grow where you live, such as specific tree, grass, or flower species. (They should be plants that continue growing or regenerate each year.) Learn what you can about each plant's dormancy and write about it in the space below.

Plant name: ....

Habitat: ....

Describe the plant's dormancy: ....

....

....

Plant name: ....

Habitat: ....

Describe the plant's dormancy: ....

....

....

Plant name: ....

Habitat: ....

Describe the plant's dormancy: ....

....

....

Choose a couple of animal species that spend the winter in your area. Learn what you can about their winter habits and fill in the prompts below.

Animal name: ....

Hibernate, torpor (reduced activity), or active? ....

Type of winter habitat: ....

What and how does it eat? ....

Other details: ....

....

....

....

....

Animal name: ....

Hibernate, torpor (reduced activity), or active? ....

Type of winter habitat: ....

What and how does it eat? ....

Other details: ....

....

....

....

....

BE AN INDOOR GARDENER

Ferns, figs, and succulents are not simply decorative; indoor plants like these are proven mood-boosters. They infuse our everyday lives with nature even when the outdoors is out of reach. When outdoor plants are dormant, start an indoor "garden" with a few houseplants. Here are some easy-to-care-for indoor plant species.

ZZ PLANT (*ZAMIOCULCAS ZAMIIFOLIA*)

- Indirect or low light
- Water when the top two inches of soil dry out (use your finger to check), about every 2–4 weeks

HEN AND CHICKS (*SEMPERVIVUM TECTORUM*)

- Bright light or full sun
- Water when the soil dries out, about every 1–4 weeks depending on the season

SPIDER PLANT (*CHLOROPHYTUM COMOSUM*)

- Bright to moderate light
- Water once a week

GOLDEN POTHOS (*EPIPREMNUM AUREUM*)

- Bright indirect light
- Water every 1–2 weeks

JADE PLANT (*CRASSULA OVATA*)

- Bright indirect light
- Water when soil dries out, about every 2–3 weeks

Whether you're a devoted plant parent or just starting out,
use the space below to plan your indoor garden for the coming year.

Location: ....

Date & Time: ....

Weather & Temperature: ....

5 Things I See:

....

....

....

....

....

3 Things I Hear:

....

....

....

1 Thing I Smell:

....

1 Thing I Feel:

....

LOOK TO THE LIGHT

We need sunlight. It keeps our inner clocks on track, boosts our mood, and causes our bodies to produce vitamin D. Yet in winter, sunlight can be scarce. When the sun *does* shine this month, make the most of it with this mindfulness meditation. Sit in the sunlight for a few minutes with your eyes closed, either indoors or outside. As you sit, imagine you're a plant soaking up the sun and simply enjoy the warmth and light. You might want to lift your head or turn your hands upward in your lap to mimic leaves. If you prefer, you can also do this meditation while facing a light therapy lamp or light box.

Miracles

by Walt Whitman

WHY, who makes much of a miracle?
As to me I know of nothing else but miracles,
Whether I walk the streets of Manhattan,
Or dart my sight over the roofs of houses toward the sky,
Or wade with naked feet along the beach just in the edge of
   the water,
Or stand under trees in the woods,
Or talk by day with any one I love, or sleep in the bed at night
with any one I love,
Or sit at table at dinner with the rest,
Or look at strangers opposite me riding in the car,
Or watch honey-bees busy around the hive of a summer forenoon,
Or animals feeding in the fields,
Or birds, or the wonderfulness of insects in the air,
Or the wonderfulness of the sundown, or of stars shining so quiet
   and bright,
Or the exquisite delicate thin curve of the new moon in spring;
These with the rest, one and all, are to me miracles,
The whole referring, yet each distinct and in its place.

To me every hour of the light and dark is a miracle,
Every cubic inch of space is a miracle,
Every square yard of the surface of the earth is spread with the same,
Every foot of the interior swarms with the same.

To me the sea is a continual miracle,
The fishes that swim—the rocks—the motion of the waves—
the ships with men in them,
What stranger miracles are there?

Think about the ways you've experienced nature this month.
Pick an experience or something you observed and use it to
inspire your own poem below.

....

....

....

....

....

....

....

....

....

....

....

....

....

....

....

....

....

....

....

....

February

"The stars awaken a certain reverence, because though always present, they are inaccessible."

–Ralph Waldo Emerson

SEEING STARS (AND PLANETS)

Winter darkness arrives early, a purple dusk seeping into the sky even before the workday ends. After sunset, time seems to contract, dinner collapsing into bedtime. Where I live, this early darkness often keeps people indoors for the night, burrowed like bears in their dens; not many people think of winter evenings as a time to enjoy the outdoors. But if we always spend the year's darker, colder evenings inside, we miss opportunities to see the wonders above us: the moon, planets, and the ancient star patterns telling stories in the sky.

To many creatures, a starry night sky isn't decorative—it's a compass and map. Sea turtle hatchlings use the moon's reflection on the water to find the ocean. The indigo bunting, a vivid blue songbird, relies on the North Star and its nearest constellations to orient itself for its journeys north and south. (It's one of hundreds of bird species that use stars during migration.) Harbor seals find their way around the ocean at night by looking to specific individual stars, called *lodestars*. Even the lowly dung beetle uses the moon and the Milky Way to navigate.

For these reasons and more, dark night skies are a valuable natural resource, but they can be hard to find. In cities, artificial light floods our streets, parking lots, and stadiums, while billboards, homes, and office buildings glow through the night. Light is necessary for modern life, but the excess artificial light of our cities creates light pollution, a phenomenon that wreaks havoc on animal life by eliminating natural darkness and obscuring the stars. Look at the night sky in most cities and you'll see a dull haze where the stars should be: a disappearing act of our own creation.

But solutions are at hand. Light pollution is caused by the overuse and misuse of artificial light. Think of billboards that flash all night or streetlights that radiate light in all directions instead of focusing it only on the ground where it's needed. Since the 1980s, the International Dark-Sky Association, a nonprofit founded by two astronomers, has been educating the public about the hazards of light pollution and the ways that communities and individuals can be part of the solution. Some actions are simple, like closing curtains at night to keep light indoors or using timers and motion sensors to limit outdoor lighting. Other solutions, like city ordinances, take more collaboration and public support.

But we don't need to wait until light pollution is solved before we can explore the night sky. In fact, maybe learning basic astronomy can help us understand why the issue of light pollution is so important. To start, we need to expand our sky search to include celestial objects that can be more easily seen in cities, like the moon, planets, star clusters, satellites, even the International Space Station (which looks a bit like a star itself). Unlike our ancestors and animal neighbors, we no longer need the moon, stars, and planets to find our way. But maybe we need them for something else.

Orion was the first constellation I learned to see as a child, tracing its diamond studs in the velvet blue as my breath formed frosty clouds. My dad pointed out the constellation one winter night in a parking lot. We weren't "stargazing," only walking to our car. It was the first time I realized there were pictures in the sky, spinning above our heads, a connection with stargazers of the past and present. Even as an adult, when I catch a glimpse of Orion on my evening commute, stretched low along the southwest horizon, I feel awe and a sense of connection. And maybe this is what we need most in winter, as we find our way through the year's shortest days and longest nights.

Even if stars are difficult to see amid your neighborhood's light pollution, there are still reasons to look skyward. Here are some celestial sights to seek out this month:

Planets

To our eyes, planets look like particularly bright stars, making it possible to see them even when there's light pollution. There are five planets that can be seen with the unaided eye (for the rest, you'll need a high-powered telescope): Mercury, Venus, Mars, Jupiter, and Saturn. Each planet's visibility depends on its orbit, so use an app or website to tell you when it'll be in view.

The Pleiades

The Pleiades, a star cluster that's also known as the Seven Sisters, is visible from many cities and can only be seen from November to April in the northern hemisphere. With the unaided eye, most people can pick out between five and seven of these celestial "sisters," but you can use binoculars to see even more. There are more than 3,000 stars in this legendary star cluster.

Orion

Constellations can be tough to see in cities, but when conditions are right, the largest and brightest of these sky pictures emerge. With his sword and diamond-studded belt, Orion is one of the brightest and most recognizable constellations in the winter sky. Named for a famed hunter in Greek mythology, Orion is visible in the northern hemisphere during winter evenings (look to the southwest sky) and isn't visible at all in the summer.

International Space Station

If you like stargazing but want a more dependable celestial object, track the International Space Station (ISS). It appears in the sky like a tiny dim star, moving along a straight path like a satellite. Even better, NASA has a website that tracks when and where the ISS will be passing overhead so you'll know when to watch for it. Find it at spotthestation.nasa.gov.

If you manage to see any of these celestial sights this month, record your experience below.

WEATHER TRACKER

Use the following chart to keep track of weather phenomena this month. First, create a key by coloring in the dots at the bottom of the page, using a different color for each circle. Then use this color-coded system to record each day's weather. Many days will have more than one type of weather.

SUNNY	CLOUDY	PARTLY CLOUDY	WINDY
○	○	○	○

RAINY	STORMY	SNOWY	FOGGY
○	○	○	○

PILLARS OF LIGHT

It's called "diamond dust," ice crystals so sparkly and small they could be crushed gemstones. At sunrise and sunset, diamond dust can create a sun pillar, a vertical beam of light that shines upward from the sun. While sun pillars are somewhat rare, you can increase your chances of seeing one. This month, if you live in a place with cold winter weather, watch the sunrise or sunset on a day when you can see thin, wispy clouds, known as cirrus clouds, near the sun.

Full Moon

Write down the date of this month's full moon and the time when it will rise so that you can observe it.

Date: _____   Time: _____

New Moon

Write down when the new moon occurs this month so you'll know the best time for stargazing.

Date: _____

Venus

Venus is Earth's nearest neighbor and the brightest object in the sky after the sun and the moon. Depending on Venus's orbit, it's usually visible throughout the year shortly after sunset or shortly before sunrise. For about two months of its nineteen-month cycle, however, Venus becomes invisible to our eyes as it passes either in front of or behind the sun.

Microclimates are hidden worlds; they're small patches of habitat where the climate and growing conditions are different from the surrounding landscape. They may have more sun or shade or be wetter or drier. Because of these differences, a microclimate can have unique plant species and its seasonal cycles may be shorter or longer. Think of a south-facing yard that's the first to sprout flowers in spring, or a shady hollow in the woods where ferns and moss grow. Are there any microclimates where you live? Visit one of them this month and record any plant life you see.

Plant name or description	Date spotted	Place spotted

Microclimates not only produce unique plant life, they can also be home to animals that aren't found in the surrounding area. (There's a warm and dry microclimate along one of my local rivers that mimics desert conditions. It's the only midwestern place I know where cactuses grow and tortoises roam—proof that microclimates can surprise you.) As you explore local microclimates this month, look for signs of animal life. Record any signs of animal life (or animals themselves) and the dates you spot them.

Creature/ sign of life	Date spotted	Place spotted	Activity (if applicable)

DRINK IN THE WILD AIR

Sometimes getting close to nature is as simple as cracking open a window or stepping outside. This time of year, many people close their windows against the winter weather. But shutting out the cold and wind also means shutting out fresh air. And outdoor air is good for us, even in cities. According to the Environmental Protection Agency, indoor air can be two to five times more polluted than outdoor air. Whereas causes of outdoor air pollution can be easy to recognize, sources of indoor air pollution are more subtle. Cooking with gas and using commonplace household products like cleansers, air fresheners, and candles all work together to compromise the air quality inside our homes. And since most heating and cooling systems don't bring in fresh air, opening a window is the easiest way to introduce it. We also tend to breathe differently when exposed to outside air, taking deeper breaths that bring more oxygen into our bodies. This month, take a five-minute breather every day for one week, either near an open window or outside. See if you can notice any positive effects. Write about them on page 201.

notes from my natural habitat

Location: ....

Date & Time: ....

Weather & Temperature: ....

5 Things I See:

....

....

....

....

....

3 Things I Hear:

....

....

....

1 Thing I Smell:

....

1 Thing I Feel:

....

REMEMBER AND REFLECT

Nature has a way of leaving an impression on us. Sometimes it's a beautiful sight like snow-covered mountains or an orchard in bloom. Or it could be a powerful experience like watching a thunderstorm roll in from the ocean or seeing the Milky Way for the first time. For this month's mindfulness activity, recall a favorite nature memory. Sit quietly, eyes closed, for three to five minutes and visualize the memory the best you can. Try to remember sensory details. Imagine the smells, sounds, and sights of this place. Afterward, remember that you can use your imagination to return to this place when you need a mental break.

February Twilight

by Sara Teasdale

I stood beside a hill
Smooth with new-laid snow.
A single star looked out
From the cold evening glow.

There was no other creature
That saw what I could see—
I stood and watched the evening star
As long as it watched me.

Think about the ways you've experienced nature this month.
Pick an experience or something you observed and use it to
inspire your own poem below.

I hope this guided journal has made you feel more at home in your natural habitat and helped you see that no matter where you live, nature is near. Some days you might connect to the outside world one fragment at a time: glimpsing a cloud overhead, hearing a few notes of a sparrow's song, catching the scent of water, or feeling the sunlight on your skin. But I hope you'll continue to have slower, more intentional outdoor experiences too, like relaxing in the grass, learning the names of plants, and watching the moon rise on an autumn evening. Because in the end, like the grass and the sparrows and the moon, you too are a part of nature. And now that you've found your place in it, may you return again and again.

FOR HIKING AND EXPLORING
AllTrails app (iOS and Android): Includes local trail maps for hiking, biking, camping, and backpacking

FOR STARGAZING
Night Sky app (iOS)
Star Walk 2 app (iOS and Android)

FOR IDENTIFYING PLANTS
Seek app (iOS and Android): Best for quick plant IDs; also facilitates animal IDs
iNaturalist app (iOS and Android): Best for more dedicated naturalists who want to connect with others and share data
Plant Snap app (iOS and Android)
National Geographic Pocket Guide to Wildflowers of North America by Catherine H. Howell (National Geographic, 2014)
Smithsonian Nature Guide: Trees by Tony Russell (DK, 2012)

FOR IDENTIFYING ANIMALS
Seek app (iOS and Android): Best for quick animal IDs; also facilitates plant IDs
iNaturalist app (iOS and Android): Best for more dedicated naturalists who want to connect with others and share data
National Geographic Pocket Guide to Mammals of North America by Catherine H. Howell (National Geographic, 2016)
Merlin Bird ID app (iOS and Android)
Audubon Guide to North American Birds: audubon.org/bird-guide
Peterson Field Guide to Birds of North America by Roger Tory Peterson (Mariner Books, 2020)

FOR LEARNING ABOUT FORAGING AND WILD EDIBLES
Urban Foraging: Find, Gather, and Cook 50 Wild Plants by Lisa M. Rose with photography by Miriam Doan (Timber Press, 2022)
Falling Fruit: A massive, collaborative map of the urban harvest, searchable by address; fallingfruit.org
Alan Bergo: foragerchef.com
Alexis Nikole Nelson: @alexisnikole on TikTok; @blackforager on Instagram, YouTube, and Twitter

Full Library of Congress Cataloging-in-Publication Data available upon request.

ISBN: 978-1-68369-343-7

Printed in China

Typeset in Aesthet Nova, Caveat, Circe, and FreightText Pro

Designed by Paige Graff
Production management by John J. McGurk

"What I Would Like to Grow in My Garden" copyright © 2018 by Katherine Riegel. Used with permission of the author. This poem originally appeared in *Tin House*, Spring 2018. "Homeopathic" copyright © 2008 by Frank X Walker. Used with permission of the author. This poem originally appeared in *Ecotone*, Spring 2008. "Poem Beginning with a Line from It's the Great Pumpkin, Charlie Brown" copyright © 2018 by Maggie Smith. Used with permission of the author. This poem originally appeared in *The Southern Review*, Summer 2018.

Stock illustrations from Basia Stryjecka, ClayStudio, Lena Nikolaeva, and Venimo

Quirk Books
215 Church Street
Philadelphia, PA 19106
quirkbooks.com

10 9 8 7 6 5 4 3 2 1